Welcome to xtb Issue Six

Footprints

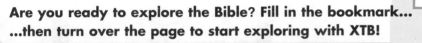

XTB stands for **eXplore The Bible**.

Read a bit of the Bible each day and...
- Zoom in on **Mark** to meet Jesus, the promised King.
- Cross into the Promised Land with **Joshua**—where battles await!
- Read the end of Paul's prison letter to the **Ephesians**.

Are you ready to explore the Bible? Fill in the bookmark...
...then turn over the page to start exploring with XTB!

Table Talk FOR FAMILIES

Look out for **Table Talk** — a book to help children and adults explore the Bible together. It can be used by:

- Families
- One adult with one child
- Children's leaders with their groups
- Any other way you want to try

Table Talk uses the same Bible passages as XTB so that they can be used together if wanted. You can buy Table Talk from your local Christian bookshop—or call us on **0845 225 0880** to order a copy.

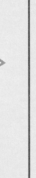

This book belongs to

....

Sometimes I'm called

.... **(nickname)**

My birthday is

....

My age is

....

Draw your
footprint
her

D0228190

OLD TESTAMENT	NEW TESTAMENT
Genesis	Matthew
Exodus	**Mark**
Leviticus	Luke
Numbers	John
Deuteronomy	Acts
Joshua	Romans
Judges	1 Corinthians
Ruth	2 Corinthians
1 Samuel	Galatians
2 Samuel	**Ephesians**
1 Kings	Philippians
2 Kings	Colossians
1 Chronicles	1 Thessalonians
2 Chronicles	2 Thessalonians
Ezra	1 Timothy
Nehemiah	2 Timothy
Esther	Titus
Job	Philemon
Psalms	Hebrews
Proverbs	James
Ecclesiastes	1 Peter
Song of Solomon	2 Peter
Isaiah	1 John
Jeremiah	2 John
Lamentations	3 John
Ezekiel	Jude
Daniel	Revelation
Hosea	
Joel	
Amos	
Obadiah	
Jonah	
Micah	
Nahum	
Habakkuk	
Zephaniah	
Haggai	
Zechariah	
Malachi	

How to find your way around the Bible

**Look out for the READ sign.
It tells you what Bible bit to read.**

**READ
Mark 4v35-41**

**So, if the notes say... READ Mark 4v35-41
...this means chapter 4 and verses 35 to 41
...and this is how you find it.**

Use the **Contents** page in your Bible to find where Mark begins

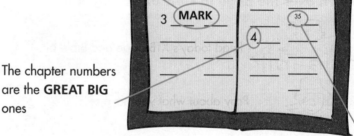

The chapter numbers are the **GREAT BIG** ones

The verse numbers are the tiny ones!

**Oops! Keep getting lost?
Cut out this bookmark and use it to keep your place.**

How to use xtb

1. Find a time and place when you can read the Bible each day.

2.  Get your Bible, a pencil and your XTB notes.

3.  Ask God to help you to understand what you read.

4. 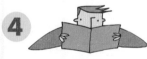 Read today's XTB page and Bible bit.

5.  Pray about what you have read and learnt.

6.  If you can, talk to an adult or a friend about what you've learnt.

YOUR FREE XTB FOOTPRINT PAD

This copy of XTB comes with a free **Footprint Notepad**.

Living for God, and putting Him <u>first</u> in your life, is sometimes called "walking in God's ways". That's what we'll be thinking about in this issue of XTB. We'll use the footprints to help us remember what we discover about "walking God's way".

And we've added some <u>extra</u> footprints for you to use however you like.

Are you ready to start? Then hurry on to Day 1.

ON YOUR MARKS

The Book of Mark

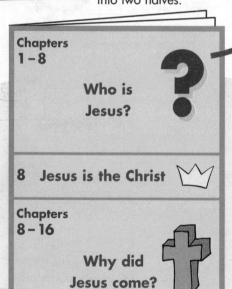

In Issue Five of **XTB** (The Promise Keeper), we started Mark's book about Jesus. It's divided into two halves:

Chapters 1–8

Who is Jesus?

8   Jesus is the Christ

Chapters 8–16

Why did Jesus come?

In the first half of his book (chapters 1–8), Mark shows us <u>who</u> Jesus is. He shows us Jesus' amazing **authority**. (*That means Jesus is in charge.*) Mark shows us that Jesus has the same authority as **God**—evidence that Jesus **is** the Son of God.

Take the first letter of each picture to see what kind of authority Jesus has.

JESUS' AUTHORITY

Jesus is in charge—He has the same authority as God.

Authority over _ _ _ _ _ _ (Mark 1v20)

Authority as a _ _ _ _ _ _ _ (Mark 1v22)

Authority over _ _ _ _ _ _ _ _ _ _ _ (Mark 1v26)

Authority over _ _ _ _ _ _ _ _ _ (Mark 1v31)

Authority to _ _ _ _ _ _ _ _ _ _ (Mark 2v5)

Today's story shows another kind of authority...

WHO IS THIS?

TERRIFIED

The Sea of Galilee is well known for its violent storms. One of them suddenly blew up while Jesus and His disciples were crossing the sea...

READ
Mark 4v35-41

The storm was **terrifying**. But where was Jesus? (v38)

The disciples woke Him up, and rudely accused Him of *not caring* about them!

> Don't you care If we drown?

STILL TERRIFIED

Jesus stood up in the boat, and <u>spoke</u> to the storm! What happened? (v39)

a) Nothing!

b) The storm got worse.

c) The wind died down and the sea was calm.

Then Jesus turned to His disciples.

> Why are you so afraid? Do you still have no
> **f_____** ? (v40)

Faith means trust.

But now the disciples were even more terrified! Of Jesus!

WHO IS THIS?

What did the disciples ask? (v41)

W____ is this? Even the **w_____** and the **w_____** obey Him!

THINK SPOT

How would <u>you</u> answer their question?

> Who is this?

This time, Jesus showed **authority over nature**. It <u>obeys</u> Him—because He is the Son of God.

PRAY

Dear God, help me to learn more about Jesus your Son as I read Mark's book.

Copy this prayer onto a footprint note. Put it in your Bible. Pray it each time you read Mark.

DAY 2   DEMON DESTROYER

The disciples have just seen Jesus stop a violent storm. Now, they meet a violent man...

READ
Mark 5v1-5

(Circle) the _wrong_ words. There are **ten** to find.

Jesus and his disciples arrived on the other side of the river. When Jesus got out of the car, a man with a friendly spirit came from the hotel to meet Him. This man lived among the tombs. He had often been chained elbow and foot, but every time he broke the ribbons. Everyone was strong enough to control him. Day and night he walked in the valleys, singing and cutting himself with scissors.

Answers: river, car, friendly, hotel, elbow, ribbons, everyone, valleys, singing, scissors.

Did you know?

Sometimes in the Bible we read about evil spirits. They are God's enemies, and often made people ill. But look back at the list of Jesus' Authority on **Day 1** to see what it tells you about evil spirits.

Jesus has <u>authority</u> over evil spirits. **He** is in charge. _Read what happened next._

READ
Mark 5v6-13

The evil spirits knew who Jesus was. What did they call Him? (v7)

S_____ of the

M_____ H_____ G_____

They knew **who** Jesus was—and they knew that **He** was <u>in charge</u>.

The evil spirits begged Jesus to let them go into the herd of pigs nearby. Jesus did—and the whole herd rushed away into the water.

THINK + PRAY

Sometimes, reading about evil spirits can be scary. But Jesus is <u>far</u> more powerful than any evil spirit! So we don't need to be afraid. Thank God that Jesus has power over evil.

SPOT THE DIFFERENCE

Mark
5v14-20

Spot the difference. *There are at least **twenty** to spot!*

Why are there so many differences in today's puzzle?
Because Jesus made a HUGE
difference to this man...

READ
Mark 5v14-20

Cross out the wrong answers.

Before he met Jesus, the man had a **friendly/evil** spirit
living in him. He lived among the **tombs/houses**. He broke
his chains and kept **screaming/dancing**.

Afterwards, the man was **sitting/standing** with Jesus.
He was **dressed/naked**, and in his **wrong/right** mind.

Spot the difference. *There is **one** to spot!*

Go away!

Let me go
with you!

See the huge difference in how people reacted to Jesus!

What did the local people
want Jesus to do? (v17)

What did the healed man
want to do? (v18)

Jesus told the man to go home to his family. He had
something very important to tell them now!
In fact, he went round the ten towns known as the Decapolis,
telling everyone what **great things** Jesus had done!

THINK+PRAY

If you're a Christian, then Jesus has done **great things**
for you too. Who can you tell about those things this week?
_____ Ask God to help you.

Follow the path through today's page!

Jesus and His disciples sailed back to the other side of Lake Galilee.

They were met by a large crowd, and a man called Jairus. He needed Jesus to come quickly to see his daughter. She was dying!

READ
Mark 5v21-34

On the way to Jairus' house, a lady who was ill came up behind Jesus. How long had she been sick? (v25)

_____ **years**

It was **Jesus** who healed her—not His clothing! What did He say? (v34)

Why do you think she was healed?
a) *Jesus had a special cloak*
b) *She believed Jesus could help her*

How quickly did she get better? (v29)

_____

She believed that Jesus could heal her, so she reached out and touched his cloak.

Your f_____ has made you well.

Faith is **believing** Jesus can help us. He <u>always</u> can, because He is the Son of God.

PRAY

Father God, thank you that Jesus can always help me. Please help me to have faith in Him. Amen

 Stop here until tomorrow— when we'll find out what happens to Jairus' daughter...

DON'T BE AFRAID—BELIEVE

 Mark 5v35-43

Did Jesus bring the girl back to life? (v42)

Yes / No

Wow! Jesus is so wonderful! He has power over sickness and even death!

PRAY Think of some other wonderful things you know about Jesus, God's Son. (*Look back at earlier stories in Mark if you want clues.*) Then thank and praise Jesus.

Jesus knew she was dead. He also knew He would bring her back to life as easily as waking her up!

The girl had definitely died—but how does Jesus describe her? (v39)

_____

READ Mark 5v37-43

Don't be
a_____;
just
b_____

GO While Jesus was speaking to the healed woman, some men arrived with a terrible message for Jairus.

Your daughter is dead!

READ Mark 5v35-36

Jairus must have felt awful! But Jesus said something amazing...

HOME SWEET HOME?

Who is Jesus? Crack the code to see Mark's answer.

— — — — — — — — — — — — — —

Check your answer in Mark 1v1.

But in today's story we meet some people who don't agree!

READ
Mark 6v1-6

Jesus went to **Nazareth**. He grew up there, so the people already knew a lot about Him.

Add the missing vowels (aeiou) to see what they knew (v3).

They knew:

• Jesus was a **c _ rp _ nt _ r**

• His mum was **M _ ry**

• He had **f _ _ r** brothers and some **s _ st _ rs**.

 These people knew Jesus' family—so they <u>didn't believe</u> He could be anyone special!

FLAG CODE

 = D

 = E

 = F

 = G

 = H

 = I

 = M

 = N

 = O

= P

 =R

= S

= T

Jesus didn't do many miracles in Nazareth. *Break the code to see what miracles are like.*

    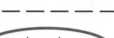

— — — — — — — — — —

Did you know?

Mark's book is showing us **who** Jesus is. That's what Jesus' miracles do, too. They are like **signposts** pointing to who Jesus is. But these people <u>ignored</u> the amazing things Jesus did and said. They refused to believe that He was God. So He didn't do many miracles in Nazareth. (v5)

How sad! These people knew a lot about Jesus, but they ignored the most important things about Him!

PRAY

Dear God, help me not to ignore the amazing things I read about Jesus. Help me to believe that He really is God. Amen

DAY 7 GOING FISHING!

Use yesterday's code to see what Jesus called His disciples.

_ _ _ _ _ _ _ _ _ _ _ _

You can read about this in Mark 1v16-18.

This didn't mean catching people in a large net! It meant telling them about **Jesus**. In today's reading, Jesus sends the disciples to do some fishing…

READ
Mark 6v7-13

The disciples went out in pairs.

Circle the things they _were_ to take with them.

They didn't take money or food. They were to trust _God_ for everything.

THINK SPOT

The disciples did what Jesus had done—healing people and driving out evil spirits. But it wasn't by their _own_ power! **Jesus** had given them the authority to do it. (v7)

Were the disciples perfect? **Yes / No / Not sure**

The disciples were _not_ perfect. As we saw on Day 1, they didn't **trust** Jesus when they were in the storm, and they still didn't **understand** everything about Jesus _But Jesus_ still sent them to tell other people about Him.

You may feel that _you_ don't **understand** much about Jesus yet—and you know that you don't always **trust** Him as much as you should. _But Jesus_ can still use you to tell other people about Him!

THINK + PRAY

Telling people about Jesus can be really scary. (I find it scary too!) But if you are willing to try, then He will use _you_ as a "fisher of people" too! **Will you?** Talk to Him about it now, and ask Him to help.

Draw a fishing net on a footprint note to remind you of your prayer.

FEAST FOR A BAD KING

In chapter six, Mark tells us about **two kings** and **two feasts**. Today, we'll read about bad *King Herod*, and his drunken feast. Tomorrow, the story moves on to good *King Jesus*, who gives a feast for thousands.

King Herod had heard about Jesus, and how His disciples were telling people all about Him...

READ
Mark 6v14-16

Who did Herod think Jesus was? (v16)

J_____ the B_____

This was because of something that happened earlier at one of Herod's feasts...

Herod **arrested** John because John told him he was disobeying God (by marrying his brother's wife).

Herod liked to listen to John.

But Herod's wife **hated** John.

Then Herod had a great feast for his birthday.

His wife's daughter danced for him.

Herod liked it, and promised her anything she wanted.

She asked for John to be killed!

So Herod had John executed. And John's followers buried him in a tomb.

Herod had John killed because of his foolish promise at the feast. Later, when Herod heard about **Jesus**, he thought it meant that John was <u>alive</u> again. But he was <u>very</u> wrong!

THINK + PRAY

Sadly, many people are still very wrong about Jesus today. They think He was just a good man, or that He didn't even exist! They don't understand <u>who</u> Jesus is. **Think** of someone you know who doesn't understand who Jesus is. **Ask God** to help them to see the <u>truth</u> about Jesus.

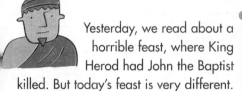

DAY 9 FEAST FOR A GOOD KING

Mark 6v30-44

Yesterday, we read about a horrible feast, where King Herod had John the Baptist killed. But today's feast is very different. It's being hosted by **King Jesus!**

When the twelve disciples returned from telling people about Jesus, many people came with them. So they got into a boat with Jesus, to go somewhere quieter.

But the crowd knew where they were going, and ran on ahead of them.

When the boat landed, thousands of people were waiting for them. So Jesus began to teach the crowds...

READ
Mark 6v34-44

How many loaves? (v38)

How many fish? (v38)

How many men ate? (v44)

If you'd been there, how would you have felt?

How many basketfuls left over? (v43)

Did you know?

They only counted **men** in the crowd. If you add the women and children Jesus probably fed over 15,000 people!

Jesus <u>taught</u> the crowds, and then <u>fed</u> them. What a great King He is!

PRAY

<u>Nothing</u> is impossible for Jesus our great King! That means that even the biggest problem is **no problem** for Jesus. Thank Him for this, and ask Him to help you with any problems you are worried about.

DAY 10

Mark
6v45-52

Crack the code to see what today's title is.

Can you guess from the title what the story is? Read the verses to find out if you're right.

READ
Mark 6v45-52

Now look again at the seven pictures in the code. Can you see where each one fits in the story?

How did the disciples feel about what Jesus did? (v51)

A_____

A ≈

E

K 💬

L ✄

R 🧔

T 👳

W 💪

 Next time you have a bath, try <u>standing</u> on the water instead of getting into it. Will you be able to???

But Jesus <u>was</u> able to stand (and walk) on water! Why? *Try explaining it in your own words:*

> Jesus could walk on water because...

As we saw on Day Six, miracles are like <u>signposts</u> pointing to **who Jesus is**. They show that Jesus can do all the same things that **God** can do, because **Jesus is the Son of God**. But the disciples haven't understood that yet. That's why they were so amazed (v52).

THINK + PRAY

In v50, Jesus told the disciples not to be afraid. Think again about **who** Jesus is. Why should that help you not to be afraid?

Jesus is **always** able to help us—and He **never** lets us down. *Write this on a footprint note. Put it somewhere you'll see it every day.* <u>Thank Jesus</u> for being like this.

DAY 11 **MIRACLE MAN**

In chapters four, five and six of Mark's book we've read about **six** miracles. Can you put them in the correct order? (*Answers at the bottom of the page.*) The first is done for you.

1
2
3
4
5
6

A Jesus fed a huge crowd.

B Jesus healed a sick lady.

C Jesus stopped a storm.

D Jesus drove out evil spirits.

E Jesus brought a girl back to life.

F Jesus walked on water.

What amazing miracles! It's not surprising that the news about Jesus spread ahead of Him. People rushed to see Him...

READ Mark 6v53-56

What did the people want to touch? (v56)

Does that remind you of one of Jesus' miracles?

The sick lady in Chapter Five (Day 4) touched Jesus' cloak and was healed. But remember—it was **Jesus** who healed her, not His clothing!

Jesus' miracles are like **signposts**. *Cross out the X's to see what they point to.*

XJEXXSXUSXXIXSXXTHXEX
XSXXONXXOXXFXGOXXDX

The people who rushed to see Jesus wanted Him to <u>heal</u> them. But, as we'll see in the next few days, Jesus came to do something far more important than healing people.

THINK + PRAY

Mark wrote his book to help us to see clearly **who** Jesus is and to **believe** in Him. Has reading Mark's book helped you to understand more about Jesus and believe in Him? If it has, then thank God.

FIT FOR THE QUEEN?

Joe and Sarah have been chosen to meet the Queen when she opens their new school. *Imagine what they are thinking, and write it in the bubbles.*

Sarah and Joe look clean and smart in their new uniforms. They look *fit for the Queen*. But what if they are really thinking, "What a stupid old bat!", "The Queen is so boring."!!! Are they <u>really</u> fit for the Queen?

FIT FOR GOD?

For hundreds of years, the religious leaders had made rules for Jewish people to keep. They believed that keeping these traditional rules made them *fit for God*.

One of those rules said you must wash your hands in a special way before eating. If you <u>didn't</u>, you were "unclean" (<u>not</u> fit for God).

READ
Mark 7v1-8

What did the disciples do? (v2)

Their hands weren't dirty! But they hadn't washed in the special way the religious leaders said they must.

Jesus called the religious leaders *hypocrites*. (That means someone who <u>says</u> one thing but <u>does</u> another.) Then Jesus quoted an Old Testament writer called Isaiah.

Fill in the gaps.

hearts   far   words

They honour me with
their **w**_____, but
their **h**_____
are **f**_____ from me. (v6)

Keeping rules made them look OK on the <u>outside</u>, but on the <u>inside</u> they weren't fit for God at all!

THINK+PRAY

Do you ever tell lies? Are you greedy, or unkind? These things come from <u>inside</u>, from our *hearts*. Tell God you are sorry. Ask Him to help you change.

DAY 13   HEART DISEASE

All of our hearts are like this. We **all** have Heart Disease.

Nothing outside you can make you

 __ __ __ __ __ __ __ by going

 __ __ __ __ you. It is what comes __ __ __ of you that makes you 'unclean'. (v15)

Wow! That was a shock to the religious leaders! They thought that what you <u>ate</u>, (and <u>washing</u> in a special way first), were the kind of things that made you **fit for God** ('clean'). But Jesus said it isn't about what you <u>do</u>—but about what's <u>inside</u> you.

The disciples were shocked too. They asked Jesus to explain...

READ
Mark 7v14-23

The long list in verses 21-22 shows what we're really like <u>inside</u>. (If you're not sure what all the words mean, ask an older person, or check in a dictionary.)

HEART CODE

 = A

= C

 = E

 = I

 = J

= L

 = N

= O

 = S

= T

= U

That's a **huge** problem! If our body is dirty, we can wash it. But we <u>can't</u> wash our hearts clean!

Who is the only person who <u>can</u> wash your heart?

__ __ __ __ __

To find out more, read **Cleaning Up** *on the next page.*

Being <u>forgiven</u> is like being <u>washed clean</u> on the inside.
- Have **you** been forgiven by Jesus?
- Do you **want** to be?
  (If you're not sure, read **Cleaning Up** again.)

PRAY   **Father God, thank you that You love me so much that You sent Jesus to rescue me. Amen**

CLEANING UP

If you looked in a mirror, and saw mud on your cheek, you'd wash it off!

But imagine a mirror that shows what you're like <u>inside</u>. Not your bones and muscles!—but what kind of person you are. It would show good things, but it would also show the things you're ashamed of—greed, selfishness, lying...

We're <u>all</u> like this inside. We all **sin**. We do what <u>we</u> want instead of what <u>God</u> wants. We'd love to be able to wash these wrong things away—just like the mud—but we **can't**.

And that's a huge problem, because sin gets in the way between us and God. It stops us from knowing Him and stops us from being His friends.

JESUS IS OUR RESCUER

But the great news is that Jesus came to **rescue** us from our sins!

How did Jesus rescue us?

At the first Easter, when Jesus was about 33 years old, He was crucified. He was nailed to a cross and left to die.

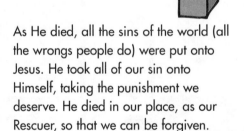

As He died, all the sins of the world (all the wrongs people do) were put onto Jesus. He took all of our sin onto Himself, taking the punishment we deserve. He died in our place, as our Rescuer, so that we can be forgiven.

Did you know?

Jesus died on the cross as our Rescuer—but He didn't stay dead! After three days, God brought Him back to life! Jesus is still alive today, ruling as our King.

Being forgiven is like being washed clean on the inside!

When Jesus died, He dealt with the problem of sin. That means there is <u>nothing</u> to separate us from God any more. That's great news for you and me!

We can know God today as our Friend and King—and one day live in heaven with Him for ever.

Have YOU been rescued by Jesus? Turn to the next page to find out more...

AM I A CHRISTIAN?

Not sure if you're a Christian? Then check it out below...

> **Christians are people who have been rescued by Jesus and follow Him as King.**

> **You can't become a Christian by trying to be good.**

That's great news, since you can't be totally good all the time!

It's about accepting what Jesus did on the cross to rescue you. To do that, you will need to **ABCD**.

A **Admit** your sin—that you do, say and think wrong things. Tell God you are sorry. Ask Him to forgive you, and to help you to change. There will be some wrong things you have to stop doing.

B **Believe** that Jesus died for you, to take the punishment for your sin; that He came back to life, and that He is still alive today.

C **Consider** the cost of living like God's friend from now on, with Him in charge. It won't be easy. Ask God to help you do this.

D **Do** something about it! In the past you've gone your own way rather than God's way. Will you hand control of your life over to Him from now on? If you're ready to ABCD, then talk to God now. The prayer will help you.

> **Jesus welcomes <u>everyone</u> who comes to Him. If you have put your trust in Him, He has rescued you from your sins and will help you to live for Him. That's great news!**

DAY 14 JESUS IS...

We're nearly half way through Mark's book. Let's remind ourselves of what he's told us so far... (*Take the first letter of each picture.*)

Jesus is the _ _ _   _ _   _ _ _

Jesus can do all the same things that <u>God</u> can do, because He is the <u>Son of God</u>. (*There's a list of some of these on Day 1.*)

Jesus is the <u>only</u> one who can

_ _ _ _ _   _ _ _   _ _ _ _   _ _ _ _ _

As we saw yesterday, Jesus came as our <u>Rescuer</u>, so that we can be forgiven.

Jump back to the beginning of Mark's book, to see what else He tells us about Jesus.

READ Mark 1v1

Jesus is the <u>Christ</u> (Messiah). This name means

_ _ _ ' _   _ _ _ _ _   _ _ _ _

The Old Testament is full of promises to the Jewish people saying that God will send them a new King, called the Messiah (or Christ).

> Does that mean Jesus came only for Jewish people?

That's what the religious leaders believed. But the next few stories in Mark's book happened where the **Gentiles** (non-Jews) lived. We're going to see that Jesus came to be King for **everyone**.

PRAY

Jesus is the Son of God, the promised King and the <u>only</u> one who can wash our hearts clean from sin. Thank and praise Jesus for being so wonderful.

DOG FOOD

Jesus is the ☐ ☐ ☐ ☐ ☐ ☐ ☐ ☐

Jesus is the promised King—the Christ (Messiah). But these promises <u>weren't</u> just for the Jews! 2000 years earlier, God had told Abraham that someone from his family would be God's way of blessing the <u>whole</u> world. That person is **Jesus!**

In today's story we meet a Greek woman. She isn't Jewish—she's a Gentile—but she believes that Jesus can help <u>her</u> too...

READ
Mark 7v24-30

What was the woman's problem? (v25)

Her daughter had

What did Jesus say to her? (v27)

Let the **c**_____ be fed first. It isn't right to take the children's food and throw it to the **d**_____.

Did you know?

Jewish people were sometimes called the ***children*** of Israel. But Gentiles (non-Jews) were rudely called ***dogs***!

But Jesus wasn't being rude! He was testing her faith in Him, as we'll see...

What did the woman reply? (v28)

Even the dogs under the **t**_____ eat the children's _____

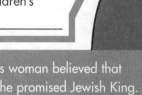

Wow! This woman believed that Jesus was the promised Jewish King. But she believed that He could help <u>her</u> too (*just like a dog gets to eat the crumbs*). And she was right! Jesus healed her daughter.

PRAY

Jesus came for Jews <u>and</u> Gentiles. Thank God that Jesus came for EVERYONE.

DAY 16 SEE HEAR!

Hundreds of years before Jesus was born, an Old Testament writer called Isaiah wrote about the promised King—the **Christ**. This is what he said:

> The blind will be able to see, and the deaf will hear. The lame will leap and dance, and those who cannot speak will shout for joy.
> *Isaiah 35v5-6*

These words come true in today's story.

READ
Mark 7v31-37

What was wrong with this man? (v32)

He was **d**_____ and could hardly **s**_____.

How quickly did Jesus heal him? (v35)

Straight away / A few days later / Never

Look back at what Isaiah said. <u>Underline</u> *the words that came true when Jesus healed this man.*

Jesus healed this man just as Isaiah said He would. That's even more evidence that Jesus is the **Christ**!

The crowds were amazed! What did they say? (v37)

He has done **e**_____ well! He even makes the deaf **h**_____ and the dumb **s**_____.

THINK + PRAY

"He has done everything well!" That's true of <u>everything</u> that Jesus has done. Not just healing—but living a perfect life, showing us what God is like, dying on the cross as our Rescuer, and coming back to life again. Use <u>your</u> voice (either aloud or quietly in your head) to **thank Jesus** for these things.

ACTION REPLAY

xtb Mark 8v1-10

Do you remember Jesus feeding a huge hungry crowd with one boy's packed lunch? (We read about it on Day 9.) Well now He does it again, but with a few differences. *Spot* **six** *differences between the two pictures.*

Look out for these differences as you read the story.

READ
Mark 8v1-10

How long had the crowd been with Jesus? (v2)

How many loaves were there? (v5)

How many baskets of leftovers? (v8)

How many men were in the crowd? (v9)

THINK SPOT

Why did Jesus do the same miracle twice?

1 Because He **cared** about people (v2—had 'compassion for them').
2 Because His followers had **missed the point** last time! (*As we'll see tomorrow.*)
3 Because the first crowd were mainly <u>Jewish</u>. This time, there were loads of <u>Gentiles</u> in the crowd. Jesus hadn't just come for <u>Jews</u>—but for **everybody**.

THINK+PRAY

Turn these three points into prayers:

1 Thank Jesus that He **cares** about everyone—including you!
2 Ask Him to help you not to **miss the point** as you read about Him.
3 Thank Him that He came for **everybody**.

Mark has given us lots of clues about **who** Jesus is. But some people are very bad at following clues!

WHAT DO THE PHARISEES THINK?

The Pharisees (religious leaders) are Jesus' enemies. But today they ask Him for a sign...

READ
Mark 8v11-13

Miracles are like **signposts** pointing to who Jesus is. But why are the Pharisees asking for a miracle? (v11)

To t_____ Jesus

The Pharisees have already made their minds up about Jesus. They <u>don't</u> believe that He is the promised Christ—so they try to test and trap Him.

WHAT DO THE DISCIPLES THINK?

Jesus warns the disciples about the 'yeast' of the Pharisees.

Did you know?

A tiny bit of **yeast** spreads through a whole loaf of bread to make it rise. Jesus was warning them that the **teaching** of the Pharisees could spread in the same way.

READ
Mark 8v14-21

When Jesus warns the disciples about the Pharisees, they miss the point again!

What do they think He is talking about? (v16)

B_____

But they are wrong...

Jesus reminded them of **two miracles**.

When Jesus used _____ loaves to feed **5000** men, there were _____ baskets full left over. (v19)

When Jesus used _____ loaves to feed **4000** men, there were _____ baskets full left over. (v20)

The disciples had **seen** these two miracles—but **missed the point!**

Copy all the red letters (in order) to see what those miracles showed.

_ _ _ _ _ _ _ _ _ _ _ _ _

WHAT DO YOU THINK?

PRAY

Tell God who <u>you</u> think Jesus is. Ask Him to help you to see Jesus even more clearly as you read Mark's book.

DAY 19

SEEING IN STAGES

 xtb — Mark 8v22-26

Look carefully at the picture. What do you see?

Do you see two faces? Or a vase? (*You may need help to see both.*)

READ Mark 8v25-26

Jesus healed this man in *two stages* to teach His disciples something important.
*Add the words **see** and **clearly** to see what it was.*

The disciples have ***seen*** Jesus' miracles (<u>signposts</u> to who Jesus is), but they haven't ***really seen*** who Jesus is.

Today's story is a picture of that.

At first the man could <u>not</u> **s**_____. Then, he could **s**_____, but not **c**_____. Finally, he could **s**_____ **c**_____.

The disciples are like this too. They **s**_____ what Jesus does, but they <u>don't</u> **s**_____ Him **c**_____. They need Jesus' help to **c**_____ **s**_____ ***who He is!***

READ Mark 8v22-24

The man was able to see again. But what did people look like to him?

 That's odd! Was Jesus having a bad day?

No! Jesus was teaching His disciples something important...

THINK + PRAY

The disciples need Jesus' help if they are ever going to **see** who He really is. (*That great moment happens tomorrow...*) <u>We</u> need Jesus' help too. Do you want to see clearly who Jesus is and get to know Him better as you read the Bible? If you do, ask Him to help you. He will!

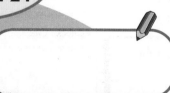

DAY 20 GOD'S CHOSEN KING

In the first half of his book, Mark has  shown us loads of ___ ___ ___ ___ ___.
These are **signposts**, pointing to who Jesus is. But the disciples don't see it yet—they keep missing the point!

Now at last, in the middle of chapter 8, the

disciples eyes are ___ ___ ___ ___ ___.
They **see** who Jesus is.

Chapters 1 – 8
Who is Jesus?

8 Jesus is the Christ

Chapters 8 – 16
Why did Jesus come?

🗡=C 🗡=D 🗡=E 🗡=I 🗡=L
🗡=N 🗡=O 🗡=P 🗡=S 🗡=U

But Jesus says they are <u>not</u> to tell people who He is—because they don't understand yet...

Like the blind man in yesterday's story, they can **see** who Jesus is, but they don't see **clearly**. They don't know <u>why</u> Jesus came.

But <u>we</u> already know the answer!

We know that Jesus came to ___ ___ ___ !
Check "Cleaning Up" after Day 13 if you're not sure why Jesus came to die.

READ
Mark 8v27-30

People had plenty of ideas about Jesus. Some thought He was *John the Baptist*, come back to life. Others thought He was *Elijah*, or one of the other *prophets* (God's messengers).

But what did **Peter** say? (v29)

You are the

Copy Peter's words onto a footprint.

Wow! Peter's eyes have been opened at last! He now sees that Jesus is the **Christ** (Messiah)—and he's right!

PRAY

Jesus **is** the **Christ**, God's chosen **King**, who came to die as our **Rescuer**. Thank God for sending Jesus, just as He promised.

More from Mark's book in the next issue of XTB.

Back in the book of **Genesis**, God made three amazing promises to Abraham.

- God said that Abraham would have a **HUGE family**.
- God said someone from Abraham's family would be God's way of **blessing the whole world**.
- And God told Abraham where his family would **live...**

> *Take the first letter of each picture to see what God promised.*

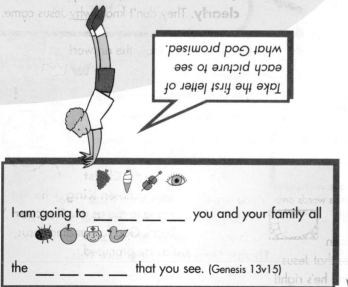

I am going to _ _ _ _ _ you and your family all

the _ _ _ _ _ that you see. (Genesis 13v15)

In **Exodus**, Abraham's family have become HUGE—just as God promised. They're called the Israelites, and there are over **Two Million** of them!!!

God made *Moses* the leader of the Israelites. God gave him this promise:

I will _ _ _ _ _ _ the Israelites from

the Egyptians and bring them out of Egypt to a

_ _ _ _ _ and spacious land. (Exodus 3v8)

God <u>did</u> rescue the Israelites from Egypt. And Moses led them across the desert to the edge of the promised land of Canaan.

But Moses died there. So the Israelites needed a new leader.

The story carries on in the book of **Joshua**. *Turn over to the next page to find out more.*

DAY 21 GET READY!

CONTINUED

Moses is now dead. But the *promise* about the land didn't die with Moses!

It's <u>God's</u> promise!—and He's going to <u>keep</u> it!

Joshua is the new leader of the Israelites. Look at what God says to him...

Get _ _ _ _ _ _ _ _ now, you and all the people 🫙🦉🐇🦆🍎⚕️ of Israel, and cross the river _ _ _ _ _ _ _ into the **land** that I am giving them. (Joshua 1v2)

Wow! God is about to keep His promise to give the land of Canaan to the Israelites!

Read the beginning of the book of **Joshua** to find out what else God says.

READ
Joshua 1v1-5

What were God's encouraging words in verse 5?

Fill in the missing vowels (aeiou).

_ w _ ll _ lw _ ys
b _ w _ th y _ _

PRAY

If you are a Christian, then these great words are for **you** too! God will <u>always</u> be with you. He will <u>never</u> let you down! **Thank God for being like this.**

DAY 22 BE STRONG!

What job would you like to do?

How about becoming the leader of over Two Million people???

Joshua has just become the new leader of the Israelites. That's a HUGE job! So God gives him some great advice...

READ
Joshua 1v6-9

Did you know?

One of the tricky things about writing **XTB** is that **you** (the readers) all use underlined versions of the Bible. Sometimes these use very different words—like courageous, determined, forefathers, meditate, prosperous and so on! That's very true in verses 6–9, so if your Bible uses any words you don't understand, ask someone, or look them up in a dictionary. *Then fill in the gaps below to see the key things God tells Joshua.*

afraid obey with strong go think time

- Be **s**_____ and brave.
- **O**_____ all of my commands.
- **T**_____ about my words all the **t**_____.
- Don't be **a**_____.
- I will be **w**_____ you wherever you **g**___.

Why do you think Joshua is to be strong and brave?
a) Because he's a good soldier.
b) Because he works out in the gym.
c) Because God is with him.
d) Because he has a large army.

Check your answer in verse 9.

THINK + PRAY

God has promised to be **with** Joshua. So Joshua really can be strong and brave! But he also needs to **read** God's Word, **think** about it and **do** what it says. (*That's in v8.*) Today, we have much more of God's Word than Joshua did. We have the *whole Bible*! Thank God for the Bible. Ask Him to help *you* to read, learn and obey it.

DAY 23 — STAY OR OBEY?

READ
Joshua 1v10-11

It's nearly time for the Israelites to go into the promised land of Canaan. How soon will they cross the Jordan river? (v11)

In _____ days time.

But there might be a problem. Some of the Israelites may not want to go...

Flashback

The Israelites are divided into twelve groups (called **tribes**). Two and a half of those tribes had already settled down on the <u>east</u> side of the Jordan river.

(They're the tribes of Gad, Reuben and half of Manasseh. Find them on the map and shade in where they're living.)

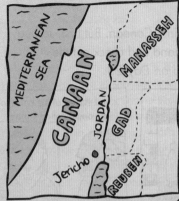

When the two and a half tribes decided to live east of the Jordan, Moses had been worried that they wouldn't help the rest of the tribes to fight for the land of Canaan.

But this is what they said to Moses at that time:

> We will do as the Lord has commanded. We will cross the Jordan and fight.

But since then they've settled down. Their families are happy. Will they <u>really</u> keep their promise...?

READ
Joshua 1v16-18

What did the two and a half tribes say to Joshua? (v16)

- We **will/won't** do everything you have told us.
- We **will/won't** go wherever you send us.

*They promised to obey Joshua and (more importantly!) to **obey God**.*

PRAY — Ask God to help <u>you</u> to obey Him and do things His way.

DAY 24 I SPY...

The Israelites are about to cross the Jordan river into Canaan. But first, Joshua sends **two spies** across the river to look at the land and check out the nearby city of **Jericho**. *Find Jericho on the map on Day 23.*

Joshua sent two spies into Canaan.

Go and look at the land, especially Jericho

They went into Jericho...

...and stayed at the house of a woman called Rahab.

The king of Jericho found out about the spies.

He sent his men to Rahab's house.

Bring out the spies!

But Rahab hid the spies on the roof, under some plants!

Shhh...

She tricked the king's men into leaving.

Go quickly! You may catch up with them.

They left the city—hunting for the spies as they went.

Based on Joshua 2v1-7.

READ
Joshua 2v7

xtb   Joshua 2v1-7

What happened straight after the king's men left the city? (v7)

The **g**_____ was shut.

The spies are safe (for now)—but they're <u>trapped</u> in the city. Will they be able to escape? *More tomorrow...*

Rahab was <u>not</u> one of God's people, yet she helped the spies to hide. **God** used this unlikely person in His plans.

THINK + PRAY

Sometimes God uses the most surprising people in His plans. But *He's in control* and always does what's best for His people. **Thank God** that His plans always work out for the good of His people.

Tomorrow we'll find out why Rahab helped God's spies.

HEARING IS BELIEVING

Crack the flag code.

The ⬜⬜⬜⬜ ⬜ ⬜ ⬜ ⬜ has given you this ⬜ ⬜ ⬜ ⬜.

The Lord your God is God in ⬜ ⬜ ⬜ ⬜ ⬜ ⬜

above and on the ⬜ ⬜ ⬜ ⬜ ⬜ below.

Is this **God** speaking?—No!
Is it **Joshua** encouraging the Israelites?—No!
These are **Rahab's** words! (And she isn't even one of God's people!) *Read the verses to see what else she says...*

READ
Joshua 2v8-14

What else has Rahab heard about God?
(Circle) *the correct answers.*

I know that God has given you this **hand/land/band**.
Everyone in the country is **happy for/terrified of** you.
We've heard how God dried up the **Red/Blue/Green** Sea for you, and how you defeated the two kings,
Simon/Silon/Sihon and **Ox/Og/Ot**. We have all lost our **homework/keys/courage** because of you.

Rahab knows that God will give the city of Jericho to the Israelites. What does she ask for?
(v12-13)

Safety for

THINK + PRAY

Rahab knew that God is **God of heaven and earth** (that means God of everything!), that He is **in control**, and that He would **keep all His promises** to the Israelites. Do *you* believe these things about God too? Then thank Him for each one of them.

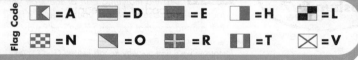

Flag Code
⬜ = A   ⬜ = D   ⬜ = E   ⬜ = H   ⬜ = L
⬜ = N   ⬜ = O   ⬜ = R   ⬜ = T   ⬜ = V

RAHAB'S ROPE TRICK

xtb Joshua 2v15-24

Think of five places people might live. (*The pics will give some clues.*)

1 _____
2 _____
3 _____
4 _____
5 _____

I'd guess that you didn't put "in a wall" as one of your answers! But that's where Rahab lived! Her house was built <u>into</u> the thick city wall.

So far, Rahab has
• <u>helped</u> the Israelite spies,
• told them what she's <u>heard</u> about God,
• and asked for <u>safety</u> for her family.
Read the verses to see what happens next.

READ
Joshua 2v15-24

Draw how the two spies escaped from Rahab's house. (v15)

What did Rahab tell the spies to do? (v16)

Hide in the hills for _____ days.

What did the spies tell Rahab to do? (v18)

Tie this _____ in your window.

THINK SPOT

Look back at Rahab's words in the speech bubbles on Day 25.

It's clear that Rahab knows that **God is in control**. But she will still have to <u>trust</u> Him when Jericho is attacked. Do you think she will find that easy? Why/why not?

The red (scarlet) cord in the window showed that Rahab was <u>trusting</u> God to save her and her family. Hang something **red** in your window (or draw a red rope on a footprint note and put that in your window). Every time you look at it, **thank God that you can always trust Him**.

THINK + PRAY

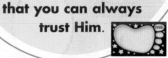

DAY 27 FOLLOW THAT BOX!

JOSHUA Chapter **1**

God told the Israelites that He would give them the land of Canaan to live in.

JOSHUA Chapter **2**

Rahab told the spies that she knew that God would give them the land.

JOSHUA Chapter **3**

Now it's time for the Israelites to cross the Jordan river into the land of Canaan.

As you read the verses, the **Ark of the Covenant** (also called the Covenant Box or Sacred Chest) will keep popping up. *Each time it does, put a tick by its picture.*

READ
Joshua 3v1-11

Put your ticks here.

How many ticks did you put? _____

Wow! These few verses mention the ark five times! (*If you keep counting, you'll find that it pops up 17 times in chapters three and four!*)

The ark must be **very** important! *Take the first letter of each picture to see what the ark reminded the Israelites about.*

_ _ _ _   _ _ _

_ _ _ _ _   _ _ _ _ _

When the Israelites saw the ark, it reminded them that **God** was with them. And that He would <u>keep</u> the promises He had made.

What did Joshua tell the Israelites?

living amazing drive

- God will do a_____ things among you. (v5)
- God will d_____ out the people living in Canaan. (v10)
- You will know that the l_____ God is among you. (v10)

THINK + PRAY

The Israelites had to **follow** the ark, and **trust** that God would do what He had promised. Being a Christian is like that too. We need to **follow** God (by obeying His words in the Bible) and **trust** that He will keep His promises to us. But that can be hard—so ask God to help you!

Why did the chicken cross the road?

To get to the other side!

Why did the Israelites cross the river?

To get to the promised land!

DAY 28 HOW TO CROSS A RIVER...

xtb Joshua 3v11-17

River Crossing Number One

*Can you find your way from **A** to **B**?*

It's hard!!

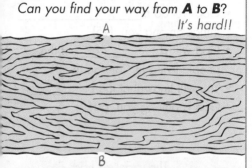

A

B

River Crossing Number Two

At Guide camp, when I was twelve, we had to cross a river using just branches and some rope. We made a swinging bridge—but it wasn't very good and we all got wet feet!

SPLOSH!

River Crossing Number Three

To reach the promised land of Canaan, the Israelites have to cross the Jordan river. It's very wide—and in full flood!

THINK SPOT

1 To cross the river in the puzzle, you had to be <u>very</u> good at *mazes*.

2 To cross the river at Guide camp, I had to be good at building *rope bridges*. (And I wasn't!)

3 The Israelites need to cross a wide, flooded river. What do you think <u>they</u> need to be *good at*?

Think about it, then read the passage to find out.

READ
Joshua 3v11-17

What did the Israelites have to do?
   a) Build a bridge
   b) Swim across the river
   c) Walk across the dry river bed

Wow! The Israelites didn't have to be good at bridge-building, or swimming, or anything! **God** <u>stopped</u> the river!!!

What is God called in verse 13?
The **L**_____ of all the **e**_____

PRAY

Our God is God of the whole earth! <u>Nothing</u> is too hard for Him! **Thank Him** for this—and **talk to Him** about anything you are worried about. He is <u>always</u> able to help!

How do you remember stuff? My dad ties a knot in his tie—and then can't remember why! My friend writes messages on her hand. What do you do?

My guess is that you don't use huge stones! But that's what the Israelites were told to do...

READ
Joshua 4v1-9

Spot the mistakes in the story. *There are <u>ten</u> to find.*

God said to Moses, "Choose ten men, one from each team, and tell them to take twelve fish from the middle of the Jordan." Joshua told each of the thirteen women to carry a box on their shoulder. The stones would help the people to forget what God had done. The men disobeyed Joshua's orders. They carried the stones to the caravan site.

Answers: The ten wrong words are Moses, ten, team, fish, thirteen, women, box, forget, disobeyed, caravan.

THINK SPOT

Imagine that it's years later, and a boy is walking through the Jordan valley with his dad. When they see the pile of boulders, the boy asks what they mean. What do you think his dad will say? (v6-7)

 They remind us of...

How do <u>you</u> remember the great things God has done for you? One way is to write them down! Write some now on your footprint notes, and stick them where you'll often see them.

Here are some suggestions of great things to remember:

God loves you.

God sent Jesus to rescue you.

God always listens when you pray.

God keeps His promises.

PRAY Choose some of these to thank God for now.

FLOODING BACK

Our XTB artist is called Kirsty. She usually draws great pics—but I've asked her to leave something important out of these ones. Can you work out what it is?

The people followed the ark to the edge of the river.

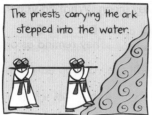

The priests carrying the ark stepped into the water.

At once, the water stopped flowing! It piled up, upstream!

The people all crossed over on the dry river bed.

Twelve men collected huge stones as reminders.

The priests left the river bed, and the water flooded back.

Kirsty has missed out the Ark of the Covenant (Covenant Box). She has drawn the poles. Now **you** need to draw the ark above them!

You can draw a simple version like this if you want. →

(It was wrapped in blue cloth while they carried it.)

READ
Joshua 4v10-18

---

xtb Joshua 4v10-18

When the priests stepped out of the river bed, what happened to the water? (v18)

_____

*Check back to **Day 27** to see what the ark reminded the people about.*

God is _____

God was with His people! (*That's why the ark is in _every_ pic!*) It was **God** who stopped the waters, and then sent them flooding back again.

From that day, the people knew that God was with **Joshua** too, just as He had been with Moses. (3v7 & 4v14)

PRAY If you are a Christian, then God is always with **you** as well—at home, at school, with friends... Thank Him for this.

DAY 31 GOD IS GREAT!

xtb Joshua 4v19-24

> The Israelites were stuck on the wrong side of the water. It was too wide and too deep for them to get across. So God did a miracle!

> He made a dry path across the water so that the Israelites could walk to the other side. After they had all crossed safely, the water flooded back again.

This dad could be telling his son about crossing the Jordan river. But can you think of <u>another</u> time when God did the same thing?

Crack the code to see if you're right.

⇨ ◁ ⬅ ▷ ▷ ⬆ ✎ ⇦   △ ↗ ⇓   ◁ ⇩ ↘ ▷ ⇩ ⇧

— — — — — — — —   — — —   — — — —

You can read about this is Exodus 14v21-31.

What were dads to tell their children? (v23)

> The **L**_____ your God dried up
> the **J**_____, just as He
> dried up the **R**_____ **S**_____.

What will everyone on earth know? (v24)

⇦ ⬅ ↘   ⬆ ▷   ⇦ ◁ ⇩ ⇧ △

— — — — — —   — —   — — — — — !

THINK + PRAY

God had dried up the Red Sea to rescue the Israelites. 40 years later, He also dried up the Jordan river! What amazing miracles! Joshua told the Israelites that these miracles would show everyone in the world how ***great God is***. That includes <u>you</u> and <u>me</u>, as we read about them in the Bible! Thank God for showing **you** how great He is.

READ
Joshua 4v19-24

⇧ = **A**   ⇨ = **C**   ↘ = **D**
⇩ = **E**   ⇦ = **G**   ↗ = **H**
⬆ = **I**   ✎ = **N**   ⬅ = **O**
◁ = **R**   ▷ = **S**   △ = **T**

DAY 32 SIGN OF PROMISE

Joshua 5v1-8

The Israelites have safely crossed the Jordan river.

The local kings have heard how God dried up the river—and they're terrified!

So, this looks like a <u>great</u> time to start to fight for the land. But there's something the Israelites have to do **first**...

READ
Joshua 5v1-8

Did you know?

Circumcision means having a small piece of skin cut off. It was a **sign** of God's promises to the Israelites, and showed that they were **His people**.

Use the wordpool to fill in the gaps.

forty
trusted
promised
desert
sign

The Israelites should have entered the **P**_____ land of Canaan forty years earlier. But they hadn't **t**_____ God. As a punishment, they spent **f**_____ years wandering around the **d**_____ instead. But now, this new generation of Israelites are circumcised as a **s**_____ that they are <u>God's people</u> and ready to <u>trust Him</u>.

Fit the missing words into the puzzle.

```
  O   T
      O   I
  T       T
          I
          T
```

T_____ **God!**

When I was at school, my friends and I wanted to show that we were Christians. So we made badges to wear saying **"God Squad"**! (*But it really wasn't a very good way to show people what we believed!*)

Can you think of some <u>better</u> ways to show that you are one of God's people? (E.g. by what you **do** or **say**.)

THINK + PRAY

The way we treat people, how hard we work, telling the truth and sharing with others. These kinds of things can all be signs showing that we're one of God's people—as well as talking about Jesus or inviting friends to church. Ask God to help you to live in a way that shows that <u>you</u> are one of His followers.

THE PROMISE KEEPER

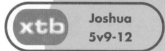
Joshua
5v9-12

READ
Joshua 5v9

What was the name of the place where the Israelites were? (v9)

> G_____

Did you know?

Gilgal means "to roll". God had **rolled away** the shame of living as slaves in someone else's land. Instead, He had given them <u>Canaan</u> to live in.

God had <u>promised</u> to bring the Israelites to the land of Canaan.

_ _ _ _ _ !

Use the flag code from Day 6.

READ
Joshua 5v10

The Israelites held a special celebration. What was it called? (v10)

> P_____

Did you know?

The Passover meal reminded the Israelites how God had rescued them from slavery in Egypt. *If you want to know more read* **Exodus 12v1-14.**

God had <u>promised</u> to rescue the Israelites from Egypt.

_ _ _ _ _ !

Use the arrow code from Day 31.

READ
Joshua 5v11-12

God had been sending special food for the Israelites. What was it called? (v12)

> M_____

Did you know?

Manna tasted like honey biscuits. The Israelites collected it each morning. God sent them manna for forty years! *You can read about it in* **Exodus 16v31-36.**

God had <u>promised</u> to give the Israelites the food they needed.

_ _ _ _ _ !

Take the first letter of each picture.

PRAY

Thank God that He <u>always</u> keeps His promises!

DAY 34 WRONG SONG!

That's a favourite song in many schools near here. But one word is <u>wrong</u>! Which do you think it is? _____

Read the verses to find out more.

READ
Joshua 5v13-6v5

Joshua met a man with a sword. But this was really **God** speaking to him!

What did he say? (v15)

> Take off your
> s_____

The ground was **holy** (special to God) because God was there, speaking to Joshua.

Did you know?

When God spoke to **Moses** from the burning bush, Moses took his sandals off for the same reason. (Exodus 3v5)

 Joshua 5v13-6v5

God told Joshua what to do.
Fill in the missing numbers.

> March around the city once a day for _____ days. Get _____ priests to carry trumpets in front of the ark. On the _____th day, march around the city _____ times with the priests blowing trumpets. When they blast out _____ long note, get all the people to shout. Then the walls of the city will fall down!

This is a really well–known story, with priests blowing trumpets, and lots of marching round in circles! But don't miss the most important point...

What was God's fantastic promise to Joshua? *Fill in the missing word.*

> _____ have handed Jericho over to you. (v2)

This is the most important point!

PRAY

Who won the battle of Jericho?
G_____ did!
<u>God</u> was in charge. <u>He</u> gave the instructions. Joshua followed <u>His</u> plans. Thank God that His plans always work out!

DAY 35 WALL FALL DOWN

WORD WALL

camp		word	
			left
	war		LORD

READ
Joshua 6v10-16

BATTLE MANUAL
How to fight a Battle
PART ONE

Make as much noise as possible to frighten your enemies
YELL!!!

But what did Joshua tell the Israelites? (v10)

Don't give a **w**_____ cry. Don't say a **w**_____ until I tell you.

Use the Word Wall to fill in the gaps.

BATTLE MANUAL
How to fight a Battle
PART TWO

When attacking a walled city, surround it with your army to trap the enemy inside.

But what did the Israelites do? (v11)

They **l**_____ the city, and returned to their **c**_____!

What an odd way to fight!

Maybe the people <u>inside</u> Jericho even *laughed* about it! But the Israelites didn't have to follow battle tactics—they just had to **obey** God!

Did they? (v14-16)   **Yes / No**

What did Joshua remind the people? (v16)

The **L**_____ has given you the city!

READ
Joshua 6v20

Was Joshua right?   **Yes / No**

PRAY

God's instructions seemed odd—but the Israelites <u>obeyed</u> Him. Ask God to help **you** to obey Him, even when that's hard or you think you may be laughed at.

DAY 36 RESCUE RECIPE

Joshua 6v22-27

Did you hang something red in your window on Day 26? What was it to remind you about?

(Check Day 26 if you're not sure.)

Use the Flag Code

— — — — — — —

The red cord in the window showed that Rahab was **trusting** God to save her and her family.

Read the verses to find out what happened to her.

READ
Joshua 6v22-27

Was Rahab saved? (v23)   **Yes / No**

What happened to Jericho? (v24)   It was **b**_____

Flag Code

| = A

| = C

| = E

| = G

| = I

| = N

| = R

| = S

| = T

| = U

| = W

Rahab was <u>right</u> to trust God! She and her whole family were **rescued**!

But we found out about something else in these verses as well...

— — — — — — — —

Joshua said that anyone who **rebuilt** Jericho would be punished (v26)—and that's exactly what happened! 500 years later, a man called Hiel rebuilt Jericho. God kept His promise and punished him. (1 Kings 16v34)

THINK + PRAY

Rahab <u>trusted</u> God—and she was rescued. 500 years later, Hiel <u>disobeyed</u> God—and he was punished. **ALL** of God's words come true. How does that make you feel? Talk to God about your answer.

RESCUE RECIPE—PART TWO

xtb John 3v16

1 Yesterday we saw that God's words <u>always</u> come true. Rahab trusted God—and she was **rescued**. Hiel disobeyed God—and he was **punished**.

So what does that mean for you and me?

W _ _ _ _ _ _ _

Fill in the gaps from yesterday's headings.

GOD
SIN

We **all** sin. We all disobey God—doing what <u>we</u> want instead of what <u>He</u> wants. Our sin separates us from God and stops us from being His friends.

2 **R** _ _ _ _ _ _ _

God always punishes sin. That means that <u>our</u> sin must be punished too!

The great news is that God sent **Jesus** to be our **Rescuer**. When Jesus died on the cross, He took the punishment that <u>we</u> deserve.

READ
John 3v16

3 **T** _ _ _ _ _ _

Fill in the gaps.

life believes die

...everyone who **b**_____ in Him shall not **d**_____ but have eternal **l**_____.

WOW!

Rahab **trusted** God—and God <u>rescued</u> her. If we believe in Jesus, and **trust** Him to save us, then He will <u>rescue</u> us too!

GOD
SIN

4 If you want to know more, check back to **Cleaning Up** after Day 13. Or, for a free booklet called **Why Did Jesus Come?** write to us at: XTB, The Good Book Company, 37 Elm Road, New Malden, Surrey, KT3 3HB. Or email me: Alison@thegoodbook.co.uk

PRAY **Father God, thank you that you love me so much that you sent Jesus to rescue me. Amen**

SERIOUS STUFF

xtb Joshua 7v1-26

God had said that everything in Jericho was to be **destroyed**, (except for any gold, silver, bronze and iron, which was to be kept in God's treasure rooms). None of the Israelites were to keep anything for themselves.

But God's rule was **not** obeyed. So God became very angry with the Israelites...

The Israelites attacked a city called Ai.

They thought God would help them win...

...but He didn't!

Joshua didn't understand what was wrong. So God told him.

Israel has sinned!

They have broken my command, and taken things that should have been destroyed.

Then God warned them:

I will **not** be with you unless you destroy those things!

Then God told Joshua that He would show the Israelites exactly **who** the guilty person was.

Based on Joshua 7v1-15.

READ
Joshua 7v16-23

What did Achan say? (v20)

> **I have**
> s_____

(Circle) the things that Achan stole from Jericho. (v21)

silver   shoes   cloak/robe
crown   gold   jewels

Achan had **sinned**—he had disobeyed God's command. Yesterday we saw that all sin must be punished. Achan was killed for his sin. That's how <u>serious</u> sin is!

If you find this hard, talk to an older Christian about it.

THINK + PRAY

Does dying seem too hard a punishment for what Achan did? That's because we don't realise how much **sin matters**. Sin is so serious that God sent Jesus to die for us, to take the punishment for our sin. *Ask God* to help you to understand how serious sin is. *Thank Him* for sending Jesus to die in your place.

DAY 39 GOD'S BATTLE PLAN

 Joshua 8v1-29

Underline the correct words from yesterday's story.

The Israelites attacked the city of **Oi / Ei / Ai**. But God was **pleased / angry** with them because a man called Achan had **stolen / given** things that should have been **destroyed / decoded**. So God **did / did not** help them to capture **Ai / Bi / Ci**.

But now that Achan has been punished for his sin, God promises to give the Israelites **victory**...

READ
Joshua 8v1-9

Fill in the gaps in God's battle plan.

- Joshua chose **t**_____ thousand of his best soldiers. (v3)

- They were to **h**_____ on the far side of the city of Ai. (v4)

- Then **J**_____ and his men would go up to the city. (v5)

- When the men from Ai came out to attack, Joshua and his men would turn and **r**_____. (v5)

- The men of Ai would **c**_____ after them. (v6)

- Then the hidden soldiers would come out of hiding and **c**_____ the city. (v7)

- **G**_____ would give them victory. (v7)

chase   hide   thirty   God   capture   run   Joshua

The plan worked just as God had said! (_That's in v10-29._)

Who made the battle plan? (v1-2)   **G**_____

Who did the Israelites obey? (v8-9)   **G**_____

How many times does **God** appear on today's page?

Circle each one.

Now fill in the gaps in the prayer below.

PRAY

G_____'s plans _always_ work out! **G**_____ is _always_ in control! Obeying **G**_____ is _always_ the best thing to do! Thank **G**_____ for these great truths about Him!

DAY 40 ALL ALL ALL

Take the first letter of each picture.

___ _____

God has kept **all** His promises to the Israelites:

- They're now in the land of **Canaan** (often called the <u>Promised</u> Land)
- They've defeated **Jericho** and **Ai**

What do you think they will do now?

☐ Have a party?

☐ Have a rest?   *Add one of*

☐ Attack another city?   *your own.*

↙

☐ _____

Read the verses to find out.

*By the way: An **altar** is like a stone table, where the Israelites cooked animals as gifts (sacrifices) to God.*

READ
Joshua 8v30-35

__ ____ ____ — ____ ____ __ ____ ___ __ ___ __

All of the people met together. They made sacrifices on the altar to say thank you and sorry to God.

Then Joshua copied something onto stones. What did he copy? (v32)

God's words were then read aloud. *Cross out every **X** and **Z** to see who was there. (v35)*

XZMXXEZXNX

WXOMZZEXNZZ

ZCHXXIZLDXZRXENX

FXORZZEIXZGNZEXXRSZ ↘

Sometimes called aliens!!!

↓ **All** the people heard God's words.

___ ____ ___ ____ __ ___ — ___ __ ___ ,

God had given the Israelites victory at Jericho and Ai—but the most <u>important</u> thing for them to know wasn't about fighting battles! It was about **obeying God's words**.

How much of God's Word did Joshua read? (v34)

None / Some / Most / All

PRAY

Dear God, thank you for your Word, the Bible. Please help me to understand it and obey it. Amen

Copy this prayer onto a footprint note. Put it in your Bible.

DAY 41 EXPLORING EPHESIANS again!

The Book of Ephesians

Who remembers Ephesians?

I do! It's a disease that makes you come out in spots!

I remember! It's a letter from Paul to the Christians in Ephesus.

No! It's a book in the Old Testament!

Who's right?

(Circle) the correct face, then check the bottom of the page to see if you're right.

Answer: Ephesians is a letter written by Paul to Christians living in the city of Ephesus (which was in the area now known as Turkey).

In the last issue of **XTB** (The Promise Keeper) we explored the <u>first</u> half of Ephesians.

 We discovered the amazing things God has done for us through Jesus.

 And using our imaginary seatbelts we explored God's HUGE plan for the universe!

Use a mirror to see what Paul wants us to explore in the <u>second</u> half of his letter.

All Christians are part of God's big plan! Paul's letter to the Ephesians will show us that God's plan should make a <u>difference</u> to the way we live.

Go straight on to the next page

DAY 41
CONTINUED

MATCHMAKING

Ephesians
2v3-5 & 4v1

How many pairs of
matching socks are there?

READ
Ephesians 4v1

Paul says that our lives should <u>match</u>
God's rescue. (Like matching socks!)

Let's remind ourselves about God's
rescue.

READ
Ephesians 2v3-5

*Fill in the gaps to see
what Paul is saying.*

You were d_____ in your sins.
God was a_____ with you
because you disobeyed Him.
BUT now you are a_____ with
Jesus. You've been s_____!

What a rescue!
*Start in the middle of the spiral to see
why God rescues people.*

That means God's rescue is a **free** gift.
It's not something we earn or deserve!

*Read along the thread to see why this
sock is unravelling.*

We can only live God's way
after God has rescued us.

And only
with <u>His</u> help!

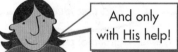

PRAY Thank God for His
free rescue!

 *Draw a matching pair of socks on your
footprint pad. Use it to mark your page in XTB. It
will remind you that we <u>can't</u> live God's way
without God's rescue!*

DAY 42 STICK TOGETHER

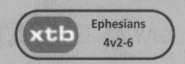
Have you ever received a present you had to look after carefully?

My brothers gave me a hamster for Christmas once!

Paul says Christians have a very special gift to look after.

READ
Ephesians 4v2-6

What has the Holy Spirit given us? (v3) **U**_____

Did you know?

Unity is when a group of people agree about something and work together in friendship.

In verses 4-6 Paul does some counting! *Write the correct number beside each word.*

Spirit	⬭	**Faith**	⬭
Hope	⬭	**Baptism**	⬭
Lord	⬭	**God**	⬭

Christians believe in the **ONE** true God and His great rescue. That's what unites us!

But the Christians below are spoiling that unity! *Fill in the gaps to show how they should change.* (You'll find the answers in verse 2.)

I'm much better than other Christians!

Be **h**_____!

I'm not helping her. She's too slow!

Be **p**_____!

He's boring! I don't want to sit with him.

Bear with others in **l**_____!

PRAY **Read verse 2 again.** Ask God to help you to be like this.

Watch out for the socks!
Each day they'll remind you of a way that our lives should match God's rescue.

God's rescue / Unity

DAY 43 GIFTS GALORE

Can you find two people the same?

Answer below.

Jesus gives <u>different</u> gifts to each Christian. (*Not the sort you get for Christmas!*) He makes us good at different things so that we can help each other.

Look inside the present for examples of the gifts Jesus gives....

Encouraging people

Talking about Jesus

Being musical

Helping people

Answer to puzzle: They're all different!

READ
Ephesians 4v11-13

Verses 11 tells us that Jesus gives some Christians the important gift of explaining the Bible. Why? (v12)

So that they can:

☐ be famous

☐ help other Christians use their gifts

As each Christian uses their gifts, the church will grow **more** united, understand **more** about Jesus and become **more** like Him! (v13)

How does Paul describe the church? (v12)

Like a **b_____**

The body will **grow** as you use the gifts Jesus has given you!

Can you think of things <u>you</u> are good at that you could use to help other Christians?

Copy them onto a footprint note. Put it somewhere to remind you that <u>you</u> can serve the rest of the church!

PRAY

Dear God, thank you for giving me gifts. Please help me to use them to serve other Christians.

Spot the socks!

DAY 44 BRAND NEW

Spot six differences between the old and new coats.

Christians should be <u>different</u> from the non-Christians around them!

READ
Ephesians 4v20-24

What makes us different? (v20-21)

truth   heard   Jesus

We know **J**_____! We have **h**_____ about Him and been taught the **t**_____!

When we believe the truth about Jesus, God makes us completely new people!

What should we do with our old self, our old way of life? (v22)

Get rid of it! Like taking off an old coat and throwing it away.

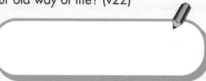

THINK + PRAY

Is that what <u>you</u> do with the things in your life that don't please God? Ask God to help you to change, and to "throw away" the things you do that don't please Him.

God has given us a <u>new</u> self—a new way of living!

Who should we be like? (v24)

Take the first letter of each picture.

___ ___ ___

This doesn't mean we can do what God does! It means our **character** should be like His, and that our lives should be pleasing to Him.

PRAY   It is <u>God</u> who changes us. Ask for help living the new life He's given you.

Sock Sign
The socks are here to remind you that we can't <u>become</u> God's friends by trying to live good lives. It's <u>because</u> God has rescued us that we want to live His way. ***Has God rescued you?*** Check "Cleaning Up" after Day 13 if you're not sure.

DAY 45 LIES ARE RUBBISH

Ephesians 4v25

Get ready to throw the old life away...

...and put on the things that please God!

READ
Ephesians 4v25

What should we stop doing or put off? (v25)

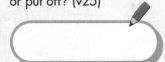

*Write **LIES** in the space on the bin above.*

What does Paul say we should do instead? (v25)

Tell the

*Write **TRUTH** in the space on the new person.*

God has made us <u>new</u>, to be like Him—and that means being truthful!

Which of these are truthful and which are lies?

T *Truthful*
L *Lies*

☐ Saying something untrue or exaggerated about someone.

☐ Admitting when you've broken something, or even telling someone before they ask.

☐ Being honest when you don't understand or find something hard.

☐ Saying you've cleaned your room when you've only put one thing away.

Think of times when you've lied. ✏️

PRAY Say sorry to God. Thank Him that He forgives us because of Jesus. Ask for God's help to put on the truth and stop lying.

Sock set

God's rescue / Truth

DAY 46 TEMPER, TEMPER

What makes you angry?

xtb Ephesians 4v26-27

READ
Ephesians 4v26-27

What is Paul saying? (v26)

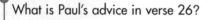

Don't **s**_____ when you're angry!

We often sin when we're angry!

For example:
Hating people
Saying nasty things
Hurting people
Fighting

Fit the red words into the bin.

H N

What is Paul's advice in verse 26?

☐ Stay angry

☐ Sort it out before today ends

Put a tick by the people trying to obey verse 26.

I'll make him pay!

Dear God, it still hurts. Help me to forgive her.

Let him feel guilty for a while. Then I'll forgive him!

I'll ring her now and say we can be friends again.

THINK + PRAY

Which of those people are <u>you</u> like when you're angry? (Be honest!) Ask God to help you to obey Him when you feel angry.

Who does Paul say we are helping if we stay angry? (v27)

The **d**_____

When we're angry, we give the devil a chance to spoil our friendships with each other and God!
So throw anger out!

*Write **ANGER** in the space on the bin.*

LIES

DAY 47 TALKING RUBBISH

xtb Ephesians 4v29-30

READ
Ephesians 4v29-30

What kind of words (talk) should we get rid of? (v29)

That means unkind or unpleasant words.

*Write **HARMFUL** in the speech bubble on the bin.*

What kind of words should we use instead? (v29)

Words that
h_____ people.

*Write **HELPFUL** in the new person's speech bubble.*

Who is sad when we use harmful words? (v30)

The H_____ S_____

Did you know?

When we are rescued by God, He gives us His Holy Spirit so that we can be sure that we belong to Him! (That's what verse 30 means.) Don't make Him sad by the words you use!

Words can **hurt** people, or **help** and encourage them.

Can you think of a harmful thing you've said? Say sorry to God, and if possible to the person you said it to.

Now think of some kind and helpful things to say to people this week. *Write them on some footprints, and stick them on your door so that you'll remember to say them!*

H_____ words.

H_____ words.

TRUTH

PRAY
Ask God to help you to use words to <u>help</u> people, not <u>harm</u> them.

Socks ahoy!

God's rescue   Helpful words

COPYCAT

Choose a picture to copy.

Draw it here. →

What's the <u>best</u> example we have of God's kindness, love, forgiveness and care?

Read along the sentence. ↓

GOD'S CHILDREN

DESERVE IT

JESUS DIED

EVEN THOUGH WE DIDN'T

AND MAKE US

TO FORGIVE US

READ

Ephesians 4v32-5v2

Who should we copy? (5v1)

How can we be more like God?

Be **k**_____ and caring, and
f_____ each other. (4v32)
Live a life of **l**_____. (5v2)

*Write **KIND, CARING, FORGIVING** and **LOVING** on the new person.*

Helpful words

TRUTH

6123714 by 51272

PRAY

That's how amazing God's love and forgiveness are! Ask for help to copy God in the way you treat other people.

1	E
2	S
3	C
4	D
5	J
6	R
7	U

There's one part of our new person in code! *Crack the code to see what it says.*

6 1 2 3 7 1 4   5 1 2 7 2
_ _ _ _ _ _ _ **by** _ _ _ _ _

It is **God** who made us new, and we can only change with <u>His</u> help. That's why the socks on these pages always come in <u>pairs</u>! *Draw a rescue sock next to the other one to stop it unravelling.*

Copy God

DAY 49 LIGHTEN UP

Have you ever been in a really dark tunnel? It's scary! It's great coming out into the light at the end!

That's like becoming a Christian...

READ
Ephesians 5v8-11

What did they use to be? (v8)

What are they now? (v8)

People who don't follow Jesus are in the <u>dark</u>! They don't know the truth about God and they disobey Him.

Becoming a Christian is like entering the light!

Light Code

 = E

 = G

 = H

 = I

 = L

 = O

 = P

 = T

xtb Ephesians 5v8-11

Christians are __ __ __ __ __ __ - __ __ __ __ __ __

*Paul says we must act like people of the **light**, living in a way that shows we follow Jesus!*

What are light-people like? (v9)

G_____, r_____

and t_____.

(Righteous means behaving like God.)

good
truthful
righteous

Who should light-people please? (v10)

Christians should find out what <u>pleases</u> God from the Bible, and have nothing to do with things that <u>don't</u> please Him (v11).

PRAY
You can't be light AND dark. Ask God to help you be a light-person!

God's rescue Light

DAY 50 BE WISE

Which would you like to be?

- ☐ Clever
- ☐ Good–looking
- ☐ Sporty
- ☐ _____

Add one of your own.

Paul says BE WISE!

READ
Ephesians 5v15-17

Fill in the gaps from verse 15.

fools
wise
careful

Be **c**_____ how you live.

Don't live as **f**_____ but as

w_____ people.

Being wise isn't about being clever, or doing really well at school! A wise person is someone who understands

 , _ _ _ _ ' _ _ _ _ _ _ _ _

What else does the wise person try to understand? (v17)

Where can we learn about God's rescue, and what He wants us to do?

In the _____

Use the code to check your answer!

Be wise, not foolish! Learn about God's rescue and what pleases Him from the Bible!

Being wise isn't just about <u>knowing</u> stuff! A wise person **lives** in a way that pleases God!

What does Paul want us to do with our time? (v16)

Make _____

That means taking every chance to please God that you get!

THINK + PRAY

Think of a chance to please God that you'll have this week. (*E.g. at home, at school, with friends...*) Ask God to help you.

Arrow Code

↗ = B   ⇨ = C   ⬧ = D   ⬇ = E

⇦ = G   ⬆ = I   ⬇ = L   ⬅ = O

▽ = R   ▷ = S   ▽ = U

DAY 51 **BE FILLED**

*Cross out the **A**s, **B**s & **C**s to see what God gives every Christian.*

1 ATHBCEABHOCCLBAYBCSAAPIBCRIABTCA

READ
Ephesians 5v18-20

What should we let the Spirit do? (v18)

F_____ us.

Being filled by the Spirit means letting Him be in control. That means we won't do things that make Him sad, and we'll obey what He teaches us from the Bible.

2 What will people filled by the Spirit do together? (v19)

S_____

The Holy Spirit uses songs about God to help us praise Him and learn about Him together.

If you know a song about God, sing it now!

BE FILLED

3 What do people filled by the Spirit always do? (v20)

T_____ God

Here are some things to thank God for. *Add some more.*

- Forgiveness
- The Holy Spirit

Now thank God for them!

4 **Every** Christian has the Holy Spirit. But we have to remember that He lives in us and let <u>Him</u> be in control.

PRAY

Dear God, help me let your Spirit fill me. Help me to sing your praise, and always be thankful. Amen

OBEY OK!

As we saw yesterday, we need to let the Holy Spirit control our whole life.

Look in the house to see which part of our lives we're learning about today.

OUR FAMILIES

READ
Ephesians 6v1-3

What are children commanded to do? (v1)

O_____ their **p**_____

Did you know?

That's from the Ten Commandments (Exodus 20v12). When we disobey our parents, we disobey **God** too!

Which four children are being disobedient?

*Write a **D** in the box beside them.*

Bedtime!

O.K.

No!

I'll ask for a drink and get an extra 5 minutes!

MUM

Bible study time!

No way!

Great!

I'll go, but I won't listen!

DAD

How easy is it to obey your parents?

☐ Easy!
☐ It depends!
☐ Really hard!

PRAY

Think about times when you've disobeyed your parents. Say sorry to them and to God. Ask God to help you to be obedient.

READ
Ephesians 6v4

God's rescue — Obeying Parents

PRAY

It's not easy being a parent! Thank God for those who look after you and ask Him to help them. If they're Christians, ask God to help them teach you about Jesus.

DAY 53 STAND FIRM

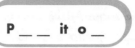

Paul is showing us how to live lives that <u>match</u> God's rescue. *But crack the code to see who wants to <u>stop</u> us!*

—— —— —— ——   —— —— —— —— ——

The devil always wants to stop us following Jesus. But in the last part of Ephesians Paul shows us how to **stand firm** against the devil...

READ
Ephesians 6v10-15

Christians are in a battle! Whose power and armour do we have to protect us? (v10-11)

God gives us everything we need to win!

 =D

 =E

 =H

 =I

 =L

 =T

 =V

What must we do with God's armour? (v13)

P _ _ it o _

To "put on God's armour" means to believe, trust and remember the good news about Jesus.

Follow the lines from each piece of armour to see what it means.

Breastplate of Righteousness

Gospel shoes

Belt of Truth

Jesus has rescued me—it's <u>true</u>.

I'm a new person! God helps me live the <u>right</u> way.

I must <u>go</u> and tell people about Jesus.

When we have this armour on, the devil <u>can't</u> trick us into believing his lies or disobeying God! That's great news!

PRAY   **Thank God for His armour.**

ALL GOD'S ARMOUR

xtb Ephesians 6v14-17

Jesus has saved us from sin.

Which soldier has ALL his armour on?

We need to wear the FULL armour of God!

READ
Ephesians 6v14-17

Faith is believing in God's promises and trusting in His power. What does faith protect us from? (v16)

The devil will try to stop us trusting God —**BUT** God gives us faith to protect us!

Fill in the gaps and draw the soldier's missing armour.

H_____ of salvation (v17)

Shield of
F_____
(v16)

Sword of the
S_____
(v17)

Draw each piece of armour on a footprint. Stick them around your room to remind you to put on the FULL armour of God.

Read around the helmet.

The devil will try to make us think that God <u>won't</u> save us—**BUT** if we're Christians, we know that He already has!

What is the Spirit's sword? (v17)

LIBBE

The _____

We need to obey the Bible and tell other people what it says. The devil will try to stop us—**BUT** the Holy Spirit will help us!

PRAY Dear God, please help me to put on ALL your armour. Amen

KEEP TALKING

Solve the code to discover the final part of a life that matches God's rescue.

_____ _ _ _ _ _ _ _

READ
Ephesians 6v14-17

In which kind of situation should we pray? (v18)
- [ ] Every kind
- [ ] Most
- [ ] A few

Did you know?

There's <u>never</u> a situation that we can't talk to God about! Talking to God about things helps us to stay alert and live His way.

Who should we pray for? (v18)

That means other Christians.

What does Paul want his readers to pray for? (v19-20)

- [ ] His football team
- [ ] A chance to get out of prison
- [ ] Courage to talk about Jesus

What a great thing to pray about!

THINK + PRAY

Pray for those you know who tell people about Jesus.

Missionaries Church leaders Sunday School teachers

Can you think of any others?

Well, that's the end of Ephesians. (_You can read Paul's "goodbye" in v21-24._) Ask God to help you to keep praying for yourself and your Christian friends as you live lives <u>matching</u> His great rescue.

God's rescue Prayer

Write the name of a Christian friend on a footprint and use it to remind you to pray for them. Maybe you could give them a footprint with your name on it and ask them to pray for you too!

BACK TO THE LAND

Welcome back to the book of **Joshua**.

The book started with God telling Joshua that the time had come to keep an important promise.

Crack the code to see what that promise was.

God promised to give the Israelites a _ _ _ _ _ _

of their own. It was the land of _ _ _ _ _ _ _ _.

On Days 21 to 40 we read the first part of Joshua. We saw how God brought the Israelites safely across the

_ _ _ _ _ _ river, and defeated the cities of

_ _ _ _ _ _ _ _ and _ _ .

The middle of the book shows how God helped the Israelites to win more battles. Then they settled down in the land.

Check out the map to see where they settled.

Flag Code

= A
= B
= C
= D
= E
= F
= H
= I
= J
= L
= N
= O
= R
= T
= U

KEY

B — Benjamin
D — Dan
I — Issachar
Z — Zebulun

Read the next page to find out more.

Joshua
21v43-45

Did you know?

There were over two million Israelites! They were divided into family groups called **tribes**. Each tribe was the family of one of Jacob's twelve sons (Reuben, Simeon, Gad etc). The map shows where each tribe settled down to live.

We read chapters 1 to 8 of Joshua last time. Now we're going to jump ahead to the end of chapter 21—which sums up everything that's happened so far...

READ
Joshua 21v43-45

How many of His promises did God keep? (v45)

None / Some / Most / All

The wonderful truth about God

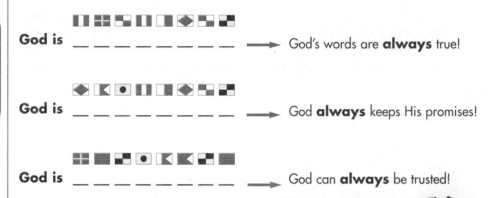

God is _ _ _ _ _ _ _ _ ⟶ God's words are **always** true!

God is _ _ _ _ _ _ _ _ ⟶ God **always** keeps His promises!

God is _ _ _ _ _ _ _ _ ⟶ God can **always** be trusted!

THINK + PRAY

Look again at these wonderful truths about God. How do they make you **feel**? (*Stop and think about it!*) What do they make you want to **do**? (*E.g. Thank Him; Tell others about Him; Sing a song praising Him; Ask Him to help you to trust Him with your problems...*)
Talk to God about your answers.

WALK IN HIS WAYS

Look again at yesterday's map. Two and a half of the tribes were living on the **East** side of the river Jordan. Which ones?

R_____

G_____

Half of

M_____

These tribes had crossed the Jordan to help the rest of the Israelites fight for Canaan. (*We read about this on Day 23.*) But now it was time for them to go home.

READ
Joshua 22v1-5

Some Bibles have "walk in His ways" in verse 5. This means living your life for God, putting Him <u>first</u> in everything. All Christians are to walk in God's ways. That's why this issue of XTB is called *Footprints*.

What were they to do from now on? (v5)

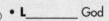
• **L**_____ God

• **O**_____ God's commands

• **S**_____ God wholeheartedly

Had the two and a half tribes obeyed God? (v3)

The second half of Ephesians is about walking in God's ways—living in a way that matches His rescue. Look back at the pairs of socks on Days 41-55 to remind yourself of what that means.

PRAY

Dear God, please help me to walk in your ways. Amen

Copy this prayer onto a Footprint note.

TRIBAL TROUBLE

The two and a half tribes set off for home.

But they stopped just before crossing the Jordan river.

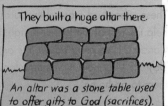

They built a huge altar there.

An altar was a stone table used to offer gifts to God (sacrifices).

When the rest of the Israelites heard about the altar they were horrified!

God's law says that we must only offer sacrifices at one place, on one altar.

They have broken God's law!

They're not living as God's people any more!

The rest of the Israelites were shocked at what the two and a half tribes had done. They were ready to go to **war!**

But first they sent 11 men to find out <u>why</u> the two and a half tribes had done this...

READ
Joshua 22v21-27

You can find this story in Joshua 22v6-20.

Fill in the gaps.   *people   worried   horrified   Jordan   not*

The two and a half tribes were **h**_____ as well!
They were **n**_____ breaking God's law (*because they didn't make any sacrifices on the altar*). But they were
w_____ that the river **J**_____ would divide them from the rest of God's **p**_____.

So they built a copy of the altar as a **witness** (sign).

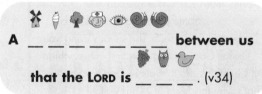

Take the first letter of each picture to see what they called it.

A _ _ _ _ _ _ _ _ _ **between us**

that the LORD is _ _ _ . (v34)

Yesterday we saw that the two and a half tribes were told to "walk in God's ways". Today's story shows that they wanted to make sure that they carried on doing that in the <u>future</u>, too.

THINK + PRAY

The two and a half tribes didn't want anything to happen in the future that might <u>stop them</u> being God's people. Do you feel like that too? If so, ask God to help you to keep living for Him <u>all your life</u>.

DAY 59 JOSHUA'S REMINDER

Joshua is now an old man. It's time for him to tell the Israelites some very important things before he dies.

Follow the maze to discover some key words from Joshua's speech.

T	I	A	F	Y	V	I
H	F	U	L	E	E	R
E	V	O	L	B	O	D
N	A	T	I	O	N	S

← →

N _ _ _ _ _ _ _

D _ _ _ _ _

O _ _ _

F _ _ _ _ _ _ _ _

L _ _ _ _

xtb   Joshua 23v1-11

Now use those words to find out the main things Joshua said in his speech. *Fill in the gaps.*

- God has fought the **n**_____ for you.
- God will **d**_____ out the rest of your enemies too.
- Be careful to **o**_____ all of God's laws.
- Be **f**_____ to God.
- **L**_____ the LORD your God.

Look out for each of these things as you read Joshua's speech.

READ
Joshua 23v1-11

Do you remember the matching socks from Ephesians? They were to remind us that our lives should <u>match</u> what God has done in rescuing us.

Joshua says the same thing to the Israelites. He reminds them of all that God has done. Then he tells them to *love* and *obey* God, being *faithful* to Him.

THINK + PRAY

If you're a Christian, then God has done wonderful things for you. (*He loves you, and has sent Jesus as your Rescuer.*) Do you live in a way that matches that? (*Think carefully!*) Say sorry to God for the times you have let Him down. Ask Him to help you to *love* and *obey* Him.

JOSHUA'S WARNING

xtb Joshua 23v12-16

God has promised to drive out the enemies of the Israelites. But they haven't all gone yet. These people pray to pretend gods (statues) instead of the LORD (the One True God). So Joshua warns the Israelites **not** to start praying to these pretend gods. If they do, there will be a price to pay...

READ
Joshua 23v12-16

Use the words below to fill in the gaps.

God has kept every **p**_____ to you. Not one has **f**_____. But if you join with the other nations and start to **s**_____ their gods, then God will be **a**_____ with you and He will **p**_____ you. None of you will be left in this **L**_____ He has given you.

Fit the missing words into the puzzle.

serve   promise
failed   land
punish
angry

D_____!

THINK SPOT · Don't get the wrong idea! Joshua warned the Israelites not to mix with other nations so they wouldn't start praying to pretend gods. He was *protecting* them.

This does **not** mean that we can't make friends with people from other countries!!! As Christians, we should be friendly to everyone we meet.

But, like the Israelites, we may need to *protect* ourselves from people who try to stop us living for God.
• Do you know anyone who makes fun of you for reading the Bible?
• Or thinks that believing in Jesus is silly?
• Or wants you to do wrong stuff like shoplifting?
If you do, you can *protect* yourself by not spending too much time with them.

If this is hard, or you are worried about it, please talk to an older Christian about it.

PRAY

Ask God to help you to keep living for Him, and not to be pulled away from Him by anyone. **Thank God** for any Christian friends who help you to live for Him.

DAY 61 HISTORY LESSON

Today we're listening in on a History lesson.
Sounds b-o-r-i-n-g? It's not!

HISTORY is **HIS STORY**.
It is **God's** Story.
So Joshua is reminding the Israelites of their history—and how **God** has kept all His promises to them.

As you read Joshua's speech, jot down the correct verse number by each of the pictures on the right.

READ
Joshua 24v1-13

Fill in the gaps from the end of v12.

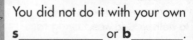

You did not do it with your own
s_____ or b_____.

It was **God** who made these great things happen—<u>not</u> the Israelites!

God took Abraham to Canaan. v	God gave Abraham and Sarah a son called Isaac. v
Jacob and his family went to Egypt. v	God chose Moses to rescue the Israelites from Egypt. v
God brought the Israelites across the Red Sea v	God won the battle of Jericho v

Think about *your history*. Draw or write three things from your own life that you can thank God for. (*Include at least one person or thing that has helped you get to know God better.*)

1

2

3

PRAY   **Thank God for these things.**

AS FOR ME...

Spot the Difference. Can you find ten? (Or more?!)

In the next part of Joshua's speech, he talks about **serving** God. But it's not the kind of **servant** in the puzzle! Or is it...?

READ
Joshua 24v14-15

Finish Joshua's words (v15)

As for me and my household, we will

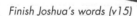

Joshua has just reminded the Israelites of all the great things God has done for them. (*See yesterday's pics.*) Now he encourages them to **serve God** in return.

THINK SPOT

The Bible uses several different ways to describe our relationship with God.

• It calls us **God's friends** (John 15v14)
• It calls us **God's children** (John 1v12)
• And it calls us **God's servants or slaves!**

If we are Christians then God is <u>in charge</u> of our lives. It's **right** for us to serve Him. And it's also a way of showing our **thanks** to Him.

Did you know?

Jesus was a servant too! Check out what He says about Himself in Mark 10v45.

THINK + PRAY

Jesus also said that whenever we serve someone else, we are really serving Jesus! How can <u>you</u> be a servant this week?

❏ Clean your room without being asked.
❏ Offer to wash up for a week.
❏ Make a cake or biscuits for someone who's ill.
❏ Clean the car (inside as well as outside!)

Tick at least two—then ask God to help you to do them!

DAY 63 YOU CAN'T SERVE GOD!

We've been thinking a lot about living for God—although we've used different words for it.

- On Day 57 we called it **walking in His ways**.
- On Day 59 it was **loving and obeying God**.
- Yesterday it was being **God's servants**.

But now Joshua tells the Israelites something astonishing! *Take the first letter of each pic to see what it was.*

_____

What an odd thing to say! *Read the verses to see why Joshua said it.*

READ
Joshua 24v16-21

Joshua is making sure that they are <u>serious</u> about their decision to serve God. It's an easy thing to **say**—but it won't be easy to **do**. So he warns them about what will happen if they turn away from God.

What did the people reply? (v21)

We...

The people were serious about serving God. So Joshua set up a large stone as a reminder of what they had said. (v22-27)

> Joshua's words are true for <u>everyone</u>—not just the Israelites. We are <u>all</u> sinful. Being sinful means that we want to serve **ourselves** (do what <u>we</u> want), rather than serve **God**.

Jesus came as our Rescuer, to save us from our sins. Have <u>you</u> been rescued by Jesus? *If you're not sure, read "Cleaning Up" after Day 13.*

THINK+PRAY

One of the great things that happens when you are rescued by Jesus is that God starts to change you. One of those changes is that you **want** to serve God (instead of serving yourself). Do you want to serve God? If you do, thank God for making that change in your life. But you will still find it hard, and sometimes you will let Him down. When that happens, tell God you are sorry and ask Him to help you to live for Him.

DAY 64 LIFE OF A SPY

xtb Joshua 24v28-31

- Like Moses, Joshua was born and brought up in **Egypt**.
- He saw the ten **plagues** and later escaped across the **Red Sea**.
- Joshua was one of 12 **spies** sent by Moses to check out the land of Canaan.
- When **Moses** died, Joshua became the new leader of the Israelites.
- God dried up the **Jordan** river so that Joshua could lead the people across.
- Joshua lived to see the Israelites peacefully settled in their new **land**.

Find all of the **bold** *words (from above) in the wordsearch. Some are written backwards!*

The left over letters spell a name.
What is it?

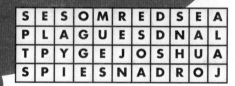

S	E	S	O	M	R	E	D	S	E	A
P	L	A	G	U	E	S	D	N	A	L
T	P	Y	G	E	J	O	S	H	U	A
S	P	I	E	S	N	A	D	R	O	J

Look again at the summary of Joshua's life, and imagine that you had been there too.
How would you have *felt* at each point?
What would you think about *God*?

Think about what you have learnt about God in the book of Joshua. Choose some words to describe Him. (E.g. powerful, faithful...)

READ
Joshua 24v28-31

How old was Joshua when he died? (v29)

Joshua had encouraged the people to keep serving God.
How long did they serve Him for? (v31)

    a) Until Joshua died.
    b) Until the leaders who had been with Joshua died.
    c) They never stopped serving God.

PRAY Use these words to thank and praise God for who He is.

DAY 65 FLASHBACK

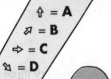
FLASHBACK ONE—Joseph

Joseph lived more than 500 years before Joshua. (*You can read about him in the book of Genesis.*) God used Joseph to save his family from famine in Canaan. Instead they went to live in Egypt. When Joseph was very old, he told his brothers what to do with his body.

READ
Genesis 50v24-26

Joseph believed that God would keep His promise to take the Israelites back to Canaan. **He was right!**

Read the end of the book of Joshua to see what happened to Joseph's body.

READ
Joshua 24v32-33

Where was Joseph's body buried? (v32)

 S _____

Shechem was in Canaan.

Code key

⇑ = A
↗ = B
⇨ = C
↘ = D
⇓ = E
⇦ = G
↖ = H
↑ = I
↘ = L
↙ = N
◁ = R
▷ = S

FLASHBACK TWO—Abraham

Abraham was Joseph's great grandfather. God made three HUGE promises to Abraham. *Crack the code to see what they were.*

↘ ⇑ ↘ ↘ → *God promised to give Abraham's family the land of Canaan to live in.*
1 ___ ___ ___ ___

⇨ ↗ ↑ ↘ ↘ ◁ ⇓ ↘ → *God said Abraham's family would be so HUGE that there would be too many to count!*
2 ___ ___ ___ ___ ___ ___ ___ ___

↗ ↘ ⇓ ▷ ▷ ↑ ↘ ⇦ → *God said someone from Abe's family would be God's way of blessing the whole world.*
3 ___ ___ ___ ___ ___ ___ ___ ___

At the end of **Joshua**, over <u>two million</u> Israelites are living in the land of Canaan. Which two promises had God kept?

1
2

God kept His <u>third</u> promise as well. **Jesus** was God's way of blessing the whole world!

PRAY
God's words always come true. Copy this onto a Footprint note and put it in your Bible. Thank God that His words are <u>always</u> true.

TIME FOR MORE?

Have you read all 65 days of XTB? Well done if you have!

How often do you use XTB?
- Every day?
- Nearly every day?
- Two or three times a week?
- Now and then?

You can use XTB at any time...

In the morning.

At bedtime.

When you get back from school.

When do <u>you</u> read XTB?

XTB comes out every three months. If you've been using it every day, or nearly every day, that's great! You may still have a few weeks to wait before you get the next issue of XTB. But don't worry!—that's what the extra readings are for...

EXTRA READINGS
The next four pages contain some extra Bible readings about Daniel. If you read one each day, they will take you 26 days. Or you may want to read two or three each day. Or just pick a few to try. Whichever suits you best. There's a cracking wordsearch to solve too...

Drop us a line...
Why not write in and tell us what you think of XTB:
—What do you like best?
—Was there something you didn't understand?
—And any ideas for how we can make it better!

Write to: XTB, The Good Book Company, 37 Elm Road, New Malden, Surrey, KT3 3HB **or e-mail me:** Alison@thegoodbook.co.uk

The extra readings start on the next page

WHO IS KING?

These extra readings come from the first four chapters of the Book of **Daniel**. In them we meet the powerful king of Babylonia. His name is my favourite name in the whole Bible—*King Nebuchadnezzar!*

Nebuchadnezzar needs to learn an important lesson. He isn't really the greatest king at all! He needs to learn that **God** is the <u>real</u> King. Daniel and his friends will help Nebuchadnezzar to learn the truth about God.

The ideas in the box will help you as you read the verses.

PRAY Ask God to help you to understand what you read.

READ Read the Bible verses, and fill in the missing word in the puzzle.

THINK Think about what you have just read. Try to work out one main thing the writer is saying.

PRAY Thank God for what you have learnt about Him.

There are 26 Bible readings on the next three pages. Part of each reading has been printed for you—but with a word missing. Fill in the missing words as you read the verses. Then see if you can find them all in the wordsearch below. Some are written backwards—or diagonally!

If you get stuck, check the answers at the end of Reading 26.

K	I	N	G	O	F	H	E	A	V	E	N	S	X	M
N	I	L	O	X	F	I	G	N	W	A	Y	S	T	Y
O	P	N	D	T	U	G	G	Y	I	T	H	A	B	S
W	I	N	G	B	R	H	P	O	D	E	E	R	H	T
L	O	R	D	S	N	O	E	N	E	N	A	G	S	E
E	A	N	I	M	A	L	E	E	O	T	W	I	E	R
D	I	F	F	I	C	U	L	T	T	I	A	S	A	I
G	X	S	K	Y	E	L	S	P	H	M	L	A	S	E
E	T	A	C	S	T	A	T	U	E	E	K	V	O	S
A	B	R	O	W	O	N	D	E	R	S	I	E	N	A
H	E	A	L	T	H	I	E	R	A	I	N	E	S	T
M	N	I	A	T	N	U	O	M	O	D	G	N	I	K

Chapter 1: Eating veggies!

Tick the box when you have read the verses.

1 ☐ **Read Daniel 1v1-2**

Nebuchadnezzar thinks he's the greatest king around—but his power really comes from God!

"The **L _ _ _** let him capture King Jehoiakim and seize some of the temple treasures." (v2)

2 ☐ **Read Daniel 1v3-7**

Some young Jewish men are to train to serve the king. They include Daniel, and his friends Shadrach, Meshach and Abednego.

"They were to be trained for **t _ _ _ _** years." (v5)

3 ☐ **Read Daniel 1v8-10**

Daniel knew it would be wrong to eat the king's food. God made the chief official (Ashpenaz) help Daniel.

"**G _ _** made Ashpenaz sympathetic to Daniel." (v9)

4 ☐ **Read Daniel 1v11-16**

Daniel suggested a test. For ten days, he and his friends would just eat vegetables.

"When the time was up, they looked **h _ _ _ _ _ _ _ _ _** and stronger than all those who had been eating the royal food." (15)

5 ☐ **Read Daniel 1v17**

God gave Daniel and his friends all the skills they needed.

"God gave the four young men **k _ _ _ _ _ _ _ _ _** and skill in literature and learning." (v17)

6 ☐ **Read Daniel 1v18-21**

King Nebuchadnezzar chose Daniel and his friends to serve him—just as God had planned!

"These four knew **t _ _ t _ _ _ _** more than any fortune-teller or magician in his whole kingdom." (v20)

Chapter 2: Bad dreams

7 ☐ **Read Daniel 2v1-6**

Nebuchadnezzar had a bad dream. He wanted his advisors to tell him what it meant. But first, they had to tell him what he had dreamt!

"Nebuchadnezzar's dream worried him so much that he couldn't **s _ _ _ _**." (v1)

8 ☐ **Read Daniel 2v7-12**

Nebuchadnezzar's advisors said no-one could tell him what his dream had been.

"What the king asks is too **d _ _ _ _ _ _ _ _**." (v11)

9 ☐ **Read Daniel 2v13-18**

*Daniel asked the king for more time. Then he told his friends to pray. He knew that only **God** could help them.*

"He told them to pray to the God of heaven for **m _ _ _ _** (undeserved kindness)." (v18)

10 ☐ **Read Daniel 2v19-23**

*Daniel praised God for showing him the king's dream. He knew that God was the **real King**.*

"He controls the times and the

s _ _ _ _ _ _ _ ; He makes and unmakes kings." (v21)

11 ☐ **Read Daniel 2v24-28**

Daniel told Nebuchadnezzar that only God could explain his dream.

"There is a God in heaven who reveals

m _ _ _ _ _ _ _ _ _ ." (v28)

12 ☐

Read Daniel 2v29-35

Daniel described the dream. It was of a huge statue, made of gold, silver, bronze, iron and clay. The statue was then smashed by a rock.

"The rock that struck the statue became a huge **m** _ _ _ _ _ _ _ _ and filled the whole earth." (v35)

13 ☐ **Read Daniel 2v36-45**

The dream was about the future. Four great kingdoms would be swept away by God's kingdom, which will last for ever.

"The God of heaven will set up a

k _ _ _ _ _ _ _ that will never be destroyed." (v44)

14 ☐ **Read Daniel 2v46-49**

*Nebuchadnezzar had learnt that God is the **real King**.*

"Your God is the God of gods and the Lord of **k** _ _ _ _ and a revealer of mysteries." (v47)

Chapter 3: Fiery furnace!

15 ☐ **Read Daniel 3v1-3**

Nebuchadnezzar built a huge gold statue, and summoned all his officials to come to it.

"King Nebuchadnezzar had a gold statue made, 27 metres (90 feet)

h _ _ _ and 3 metres (9 feet)

w _ _ _ ." (v1)

16 ☐ **Read Daniel 3v4-7**

Nebuchadnezzar commanded that everyone must bow down to his statue.

"Anyone who does not bow down and worship will immediately be thrown into a blazing

f _ _ _ _ _ _ _ ." (v6)

17 ☐ **Read Daniel 3v8-15**

Daniel's friends (Shadrach, Meshach and Abednego), were near the statue. But they didn't bow down to it!

"They do not worship your gods or bow down to the **s** _ _ _ _ _ _ you set up." (v12)

18 ☐ **Read Daniel 3v16-18**

Shadrach, Meshach and Abednego tell Nebuchadnezzar that God is certainly able to rescue them.

"The God we serve is able to

s _ _ _ us." (v17)

19 ☐ **Read Daniel 3v19-27**

The three friends were thrown into the blazing furnace. Nebuchadnezzar was amazed at what happened next!

"I see four men **W** _ _ _ _ _ _ around in the fire, untied and unharmed!" (v25)

20 ☐ **Read Daniel 3v28-30**

*Nebuchadnezzar was amazed. He had learnt that God really is able to **save** His people.*

"No **O** _ _ _ _ god can save in this way." (v29)

Chapter 4: Eating grass!

21 ☐ **Read Daniel 4v1-3**

Nebuchadnezzar wrote Chapter Four himself! He tells us about the amazing things God has done.

"Listen to my account of the **W** _ _ _ _ _ _ _ and miracles the Most High God has shown me." (v2)

22 ☐ **Daniel 4v4-14**

Nebuchadnezzar had another dream—about a great tree that was cut down, and a messenger from God.

"The tree grew bigger and bigger until it reached the **S** _ _ and could be seen by everyone in the world." (v11)

23 ☐ **Read Daniel 4v15-18**

In the dream, God's messenger said that someone would spend seven years living like an animal!

"For seven years he will not have a human mind, but the mind of an **a** _ _ _ _ _ _." (v16)

24 ☐ **Read Daniel 4v19-27**

Daniel told Nebuchadnezzar that <u>he</u> was like the great tree. If he didn't change his ways, he would stop being king and start to live like an animal instead!

"Then you will admit that the Most High God controls all human kingdoms, and that He can give them to **a** _ _ _ _ _ _ He chooses." (v25)

25 ☐ **Read Daniel 4v28-33**

Nebuchadnezzar <u>didn't</u> change. He boasted about how great he was—and suddenly found himself living like an animal!

"He was driven away from people and ate **g** _ _ _ _ like an ox." (v33)

26 ☐ **Read Daniel 4v34-37**

*After seven years, Nebuchadnezzar's sanity returned, and he became king again. He praised **God** as the <u>real King</u>.*

"I praise, honour and glorify the **K** _ _ _ of **h** _ _ _ _ _ _. Everything He does is right and just."

WHAT NEXT?

XTB comes out every three months. Each issue contains 65 full XTB pages, plus 26 days of extra readings. By the time you've used them all, the next issue of XTB will be available.

ISSUE SEVEN OF XTB

Issue Seven of XTB explores the books of Mark, Judges, Ruth and Psalms.

- Investigate <u>who</u> Jesus is and <u>why</u> He came in **Mark**.
- Will the Israelites live for God, now that they are settled in the promised land? Find out in **Judges**.
- Meet **Ruth**, King David's great grandmother.
- Praise and thank God with **Psalms**.

Available March 2004 from your local Christian bookshop —or call us on **0845 225 0880** to order a copy.

Look out for these three seasonal editions of XTB: *Christmas Unpacked, Easter Unscrambled* and *Summer Signposts*. Available now.

XTB Joke Page

What goes Squeak Bang! Squeak Bang! Dynamice!
Maggie Thornborough

What is the biggest boot in the world? Italy!
Jonathan Wintle

Why did the lobster blush? Because he saw the salad dressing.
Elizabeth Priestley

What is black and white and red all over? A newspaper!
Jonathan Wintle

What do you get if you cross a cow with a camel? Lumpy custard!
Jennie Thornborough

Do <u>you</u> know any good jokes?
—send them in and they might appear in XTB!

Do you have any questions?
...about anything you've read in XTB.
—send them in and we'll do our best to answer them.

Write to: XTB, The Good Book Company, 37 Elm Road, New Malden, Surrey, KT3 3HB **or e-mail me:** Alison@thegoodbook.co.uk